Stress to Success for Managers and Employees

A Dynamic Programme for Total Wellbeing

HANSA PANKHANIA

The tools in this book can be used in the real world during everyday activities, and throughout your lifetime to maintain a calm, productive, fulfilling and meaningful existence.

www.fast-print.net/store.php

STRESS TO SUCCESS FOR MANAGERS AND EMPLOYEES
Copyright © Hansa Pankhania 2016

All rights reserved

No part of this book may be reproduced in any form by photocopying or any electronic or mechanical means, including information storage or retrieval systems, without permission in writing from both the copyright owner and the publisher of the book.

The right of Hansa Pankhania to be identified as the author of this work has been asserted by her in accordance with the Copyright, Designs and Patents Act 1988 and any subsequent amendments thereto.

A catalogue record for this book is available from the British Library

ISBN 978-178456-357-8

First published 2016 by
FASTPRINT PUBLISHING
Peterborough, England.

CONTENTS

Introduction   **1**

Chapter One – Getting Ready for the Four-Week Programme   7

Chapter Two – The Breath   21

Chapter Three – The Body   39

Chapter Four – The Mind   59

Chapter Five – Relationships   89

Chapter Six – Why Use These Tools? Evidence and Research   109

Conclusion   **117**

Audio versions of some of these techniques can be found at www.aumconsultancy.co.uk

Disclaimer

This book is presented solely for educational purposes. The author is not offering the information in this book as health counseling and it should not substitute medical advice. Please speak to your doctor while working on this programme as the tips are passed on in good faith by the author. While best efforts have been used in preparing this book, the author makes no representations or warranties of any kind, and assumes no liabilities of any kind, with respect to the accuracy or completeness of the contents, and specifically disclaims any implied warranties of merchantability or fitness of use for a particular purpose. The author shall not be held liable or responsible to any person or entity with respect to any loss or incidental or consequential damages caused, or alleged to have been caused, directly or indirectly, by the information or programmes contained herein.

STRESS TO SUCCESS FOR MANAGERS AND EMPLOYEES

Introduction

Barely a day goes by where I don't feel some kind of stress.

It's a statement that I hear, in some form or another, from almost every businessperson that I coach. It starts with CEOs and managers, trickling its way into boardrooms, conference rooms, meeting rooms and offices. Nobody is immune and even the most resilient have their moments with it. In the more extreme cases, stress is pretty much all that is known.

If that sounds familiar, then you may have already wondered what impact stress is having on your daily life. Perhaps you have delved a little deeper and wondered how it is affecting your health and wellbeing. You may have read from time to time that stress is one of our biggest killers. But if you are like most people, perhaps you don't link this fact to the way you are doing things in your everyday life. You go home, you snap at your partner, your family members or your friends. Maybe you even tell them it's because you are stressed at work. But as a smart, self-reliant and independent person, you may have found yourself wondering if there is anything you can do to live differently.

As a matter of fact, there is.

There is a way of not only managing your stress, but of living far beyond it. There is a way of excelling at work, and life, without being governed by external pressures. Instead of feeling like your outside world has a hold on you and it is constantly triggering reactions from within, you can learn to strengthen your inner resources and respond without feeling stressed or triggered.

The type of stress management that I am describing doesn't involve exercising or going to the gym. This has been touted as *the* stress management tool in the corporate world for far too long. Yes, exercise helps with stress and has many other health benefits too. But the reality is that if you are operating in a high-performance working environment, chances are you don't have time to go to the gym as often as you need to in order to consistently impact your stress levels. The techniques presented in this book won't require you to take much time out; yet they are a quick fix to the stress you are experiencing. In addition, you can use them in short, sharp bursts to both prevent stress and relieve it.

Stress Starts in Your Mind

Stress starts in your mind. It gets held in your body, which is why burning it off at the gym helps, but it starts with your thinking. You probably know this anyway. Most of the people I coach have lost track of the number of times they have heard that stress starts in their mind and that if they change the way their mind reacts, the stress will go away. We hear this time and time again, but most of us don't actually know how to stop the mind from reacting. The mind triggers a chemical response in the body, which becomes a feeling, and then we are riding that feeling like a wave. We lose touch with who we really are and become robot-like in our reactions as a result.

You may have wondered why, despite your best intentions, you have found that others trigger you at times. The key to understanding why we get triggered by someone else lies in our past.

Our experiences have shaped us into who we are today. If some of them were negative, and especially if we haven't dealt with them, they can become baggage that we carry around with us. From our life experience we learn our beliefs about life, and they create filters through which we see the world. Our upbringing, our schooling: all of these contribute to how we filter life and reality and they create certain buttons for us that become our triggers. Someone else pushes one of these buttons and we think they are to blame for how we feel. But the reality is, they have just activated something within us that is already there.

Many modern psychological theories highlight that the reason our stuff gets triggered in this way is because a part of our brain, known as the reptilian brain, is hardwired for our survival. Stressful and traumatic experiences are stored in our subconscious mind because our reptilian brain is trying to keep us safe. It wants to prevent anything that threatened us in the past from happening again. When we see something in our external reality that reminds us of what we originally learnt, it releases a whole host of chemicals, signalling that we are not safe.

However, there is a way to change this problem at the root. It doesn't involve mind control or any weird or 'out-there' practices. Instead, you'll learn simple techniques that you can practice anywhere – when you are in a queue for a sandwich, when your laptop is rebooting, when you're sitting in a traffic jam – and these practices will have a profound effect on your everyday life. Your boss (or board of directors if you are in a management position) will pile on the requests and you will suddenly be able to handle them. There'll be a crisis at work and you will be at the eye of the storm, calm and collected. You'll go home and your partner will be upset and this time it won't push you over the edge. You might expect it to take months or years to have these kinds of results, but if you practise these simple techniques consistently, you will find that you will start to see changes almost instantly.

But I'm not just going to ask you to take my word for it. Over the past few years a host of research has sprung up around the use of techniques similar to the ones presented in this book in a corporate setting. Corporations such as Google have integrated them into their infrastructure and have seen outstanding results, which include improvement in productivity and focus, reduced stress levels, and improvement of health and wellbeing among participating employees. (We'll draw more on this research later.) So, I'm not only going to share practical tools which can be incorporated into your everyday routine and that will impact your day-to-day working life, energy and resilience – I'm also going to give you the research behind why these tools work and why they create positive changes in your life.

The techniques in this book are a unique blend of East and West. My formal professional training has been in Western psychological and wellbeing models and I have been inspired by the Eastern wisdom I gathered during my upbringing. I've coached many people like yourself in corporate settings and worked there myself. I know what the pressure is like. And, as a person of Indian origin, I have roots in tools such as meditation and have seen the effects that they have in corporate settings. Although it has become fashionable to use meditation and mindfulness techniques in the corporate world, I was doing it long before it was a fashion and have seen longstanding results with myself, as well as the people that I've coached and trained. This also means that I have gathered a broad range of practices that have been tried and tested before with great results. Some of the tools I have borrowed or adapted from leaders in the field. Others I have created myself. There is a discussion of the scientific evidence of some of these in Chapter 6.

We are going to start out with where you are now. I'll help you measure your current stress levels so that you can quantify the results you get. Then over a four-week period we will incorporate some simple tools that won't take up much time but that will change the way your whole day goes. By the end of the twenty-eight days, if you have practised a little every day, it is highly likely that you will be transformed into a calm, relaxed and resilient person. It's a state of being that you can keep nurturing beyond this programme. Later chapters will support you to integrate what you have learnt into your life, but the initial twenty-eight days will give you a really good head start.

Although we are going to be exploring the benefits of using these tools in more detail, you might be asking yourself whether this is a valuable use of your time. Maybe you are even questioning whether you can afford to fit this programme into your hectic lifestyle. I would say that you can't afford not to. The truth is, you want to be top of your game. You work in a highly competitive market and you want to stand out. You want to stand out individually, and if you are a CEO or corporate leader, you want your company to stand out too. Whether you engage in this programme individually or take it on as a company, I can say with confidence that the small investment it takes you in time will be far outweighed by the results you get. But again, don't just take my word for it. Try it out and see for yourself. If you keep doing what you have been doing, then twenty-eight days from now your life is probably going to be pretty much the same. But if you invest a small amount of time on a regular basis in doing these practices, you are likely to see a radical difference.

I look forward to sharing these tools with you and enabling you to get the results that you want. I look forward to you feeling calmer, more focused and present, more resilient and able to manage the challenges in your work and home life in a completely different way. But most importantly, I want for you to feel that you are in control of you, and that nothing in your external world can knock you off your path. That alone is probably one of the best investments you can make for yourself, not only as a businessperson, but also as a human being.

CHAPTER ONE

Getting Ready

You're in pretty good shape for the shape you are in.
Dr Seuss

Chances are you are reading this book because you haven't mastered present moment awareness yet. You've probably heard that it can impact the way you do business. Often we are shown a stereotype of Zen monks, or a yogi with a calm, serene face and it all seems a million miles away from where we are in the office. Yet the tools that they use are accessible to you and me, and can have an immediate impact on our daily lives.

We're going to start out exactly where you are. No egos, no self-judgement, no thinking you should be anywhere else.

At the same time, we want to get you ready for the four weeks to come. You already know that all good projects start with ample preparation, and just as you wouldn't walk into a board meeting without getting everything lined up first, so we don't want to start this programme without getting you ready for it.

Tests (Measuring Your Progress)

Over the years that I have done this kind of work with people, I have noticed one pattern that occurs over and over again. When someone starts this programme in a stressed state, and then they start to get positive results, they forget about how they were when they started. "I was never really that bad in the first place," and, "I've always been this calm," are phrases that I hear regularly. A similar phenomenon exists in the therapeutic world, and is known as the Apex Effect. A client might work with a practitioner and make changes and then forget how bad their issues were to begin with.

The reason it is crucial that you get clear markers of the effects of this programme is that, if you don't attribute your calm state to practicing these techniques, it will be easy for you to talk yourself out of them when you feel good. When you do this, you will probably find yourself in a cycle of doing them, getting results, believing that you don't need them anymore, and then becoming more stressed and less resilient when you stop doing them. By testing certain markers at the beginning and end of the programme, you will be able to relate the results that you get to the techniques that we practise in the programme, and you will be more likely to continue them, and even share them with colleagues or team members.

Ideally, this programme will be adopted by your whole workplace and not just you. While it is one thing for you to manage your own stress levels effectively, it is another to be constantly dealing with someone else's. Although we will give you tools for better managing your relationships with others in Chapter 5, if you can get the whole office or company on board from the start, even better. Not only will it increase your likelihood to stick to the programme, but it will increase the efficiency of your team members and enable whole team development.

TEST: Consult your doctor or health care provider before you begin this programme. The most effective test to measure your stress levels is a blood pressure test from your doctor. Get your blood pressure measured at the start of the programme and again at the end of the programme. This can be a very solid indicator of whether there has been a physiological change from the work you do over the next month.

Measures

I have included two measures for your use. The Warwick and Edinburgh Mental Wellbeing Scale (WEMWBS) and the GAD-7 questionnaire. The WEMWBS will highlight stress at the lower level and the GAD-7 measures stress at the higher level; it also measures levels of anxiety. It will be helpful to take your score at this stage of the programme, and then repeat it at the end so you can measure your progress.

WEMWBS

Below are some statements about feelings and thoughts.

Please tick (*v)* the box that best describes your experience of each over the **last 2 weeks**.

STATEMENTS	None of the time	Rarely	Some of the time	Often	All of the time
I've been feeling optimistic about the future	1	2	3	4	5
I've been feeling useful	1	2	3	4	5
I've been feeling relaxed	1	2	3	4	5
I've been feeling interested in other people	1	2	3	4	5
I've had energy to spare	1	2	3	4	5
I've been dealing with problems well	1	2	3	4	5
I've been thinking clearly	1	2	3	4	5
I've been feeling good about myself	1	2	3	4	5
I've been feeling close to other people	1	2	3	4	5
I've been feeling confident	1	2	3	4	5
I've been able to make up my own mind about things	1	2	3	4	5
I've been feeling loved	1	2	3	4	5
I've been interested in new things	1	2	3	4	5
I've been feeling cheerful	1	2	3	4	5

© WEMWBS

Warwick-Edinburgh Mental Well-being Scale (WEMWBS)
© NHS Health Scotland, University of Warwick and University of Edinburgh, 2006, all rights reserved.

At the end of the programme we will reassess your answers to check your progress.

GAD-7 Anxiety Scale

Please answer each of the seven questions with one of four responses:

Over the last 2 weeks, how often have you been bothered by the following problems?	Not at all	Several days	Over half the days	Nearly every day
1. Feeling nervous, anxious, or on edge	0	1	2	3
2. Not being able to stop or control worrying	0	1	2	3
3. Worrying too much about different things	0	1	2	3
4. Trouble relaxing	0	1	2	3
5. Being so restless that it's hard to sit still	0	1	2	3
6. Becoming easily annoyed or irritable	0	1	2	3
7. Feeling afraid as if something awful might happen	0	1	2	3

Overall, how difficult have these problems made it for you to do your work, take care of things at home, or get along with other people?

- **Not difficult at all** ___
- **Somewhat difficult** ___
- **Very difficult** ___
- **Extremely difficult** ___

Score	Severity
10	Mild Depression
11-14	Moderate Depression
15-19	Moderate to Severe Depression
20	Severe Depression

It is advisable that you seek additional professional help if you are measuring above 15 on the scale.

Prevention and Firefighting

The tools presented in this book have a dual purpose. The first is prevention. A regular practice of a combination of these techniques will increase your resilience, lower your stress levels, improve your health and wellbeing, as well as making you sharper and more focused. The second will help you to manage current stress levels or emotional triggers more effectively.

Sitting, Lying Down, Standing, Walking

In this book, you'll find a variety of techniques, from those that you can do standing up, to sitting down and lying down. There are even exercises for when you are stuck in traffic and others that you can do whilst you are walking.

Ensuring you get a balance between the different types of practices in this book is essential. If you are on the go all the time and have been in a highly stressed state for some time, then you might find yourself wanting to avoid the longer sitting or lying down techniques.

At first it might feel "unnatural" to sit or lie down for extended periods. A stressed and hypervigilant state often means that your HPA axis (hypothalamus, pituitary, adrenal axis) has been releasing an excess of adrenaline in your body. With a heightened adrenaline response, some of the techniques that require you to sit or lie down may feel unnatural at first, and you might find yourself resisting them or favouring the ones that are more active.

However, balancing the different techniques that are presented in this book is going to reduce the amount of adrenaline in your system. You will find a number of suggestions for you, particularly early on in the programme, if you currently have a heightened level of stress and find that you are experiencing unease when you approach the practices.

Tips for Consistency

In order to increase your likelihood of participating in the programme, read and prepare for each practice the night before. Setting the intention for when you are going to do the practice the following day, and even including it in your daily planner, will mean you are much more likely to engage in it than if you think about it three quarters of the way through the day. If you have not set the intention in advance, you are much more likely to talk yourself out of it than if you have planned for it. You are probably used to having a dynamic schedule and needing to shift things about, so it isn't about being rigid, but more about being intentional.

Missing a Day

The programme is designed so that between Monday and Friday you practise the actual techniques, and on Saturday and Sunday you have time for integration, contemplation and reflection. You will get the best out of this programme if you practise with consistency, but if you do miss one of the processes in the programme during the week, you might want to carry out the one you missed at the weekend. This way, you can experience all the benefits of the different types of tools that are practised during the week, and ensure you are getting a full range of experiences during the programme. For most of the techniques, each day builds on the previous one, so practicing them sequentially is preferential.

Repeating Practices That You Like

If a particular technique works for you, then you are obviously free to practice it regularly alongside the others in the programme. During the four weeks, we will be building on the previous week. The first week we will focus on the breath, the second week on the body, the third week on the mind and the fourth on your relationships with others. And I want to highlight that, although we are going to focus on each of these areas separately, they are all interrelated. In other words, each one affects the others. For this reason, it may benefit you to choose one of the techniques from each week that really works for you, and repeat it alongside the other daily practices. This might sound overwhelming at first, but given that many of the tools can be adapted to be done at work in as little as one minute, you will probably find that developing a range of tools to have at your disposal will lead to more effective results, and a more dynamic practice. In addition, although we will be touching on different kinds of practices every day during the programme, you will likely get a deeper experience of each technique every time you repeat it, so it is worth investing a bit of extra effort, particularly in those practices that are having an obvious effect.

Now that you are prepared for the four-week programme, we are ready to begin the practices. As we mentioned, the programme is designed to start on a Monday and take you through the working week, so it is advisable to read the introduction to each chapter and do the Sunday preparation exercises before the week starts. That way, you will be ready for the week ahead.

A Word About Practicing Mechanically

One thing you will notice about the techniques in this book is that they require your physical participation! And, when you do participate, given a busy lifestyle, you can end up practicing these tools mechanically. That is, you go through the motions of the practices but you aren't really there. They become another thing to do on your to-do list. You do them. You tick them off the list. But you weren't really there in the process.

There may be a number of things in your routine that you have got used to doing this way. But the exercises in this book are designed to help you bring more presence to your life. That is, you actually engage with them – mind and body – rather than going through the motions whilst thinking of other things.

If you find yourself practicing these techniques mechanically, don't judge yourself. Rather, notice that you are doing so and then bring your attention and focus back onto what you are doing. You may have to do this a number of times (even countless times) if you have got into mechanical habits in your life. But what you will notice is that the more you are able to do bring yourself back to this kind of awareness in your practices, the more you will be able to do so in life too.

So, one of the main benefits of this programme is that it enables you to have more awareness of each moment, and to engage in and show up in your life without feeling like it has become a series of tick boxes or actions that you aren't really present for. The effects will be cumulative, so rather than expecting the tools to make you instantly present, you will probably find that each day, you experience a little more presence and awareness until that becomes a state which is more normalised than any autopilot you have found yourself on.

Summary of Chapter One

Test yourself before you start out so that you are able to measure your progress.

The practices in this book are designed for prevention. They will increase your resilience, lower your stress levels, improve your health and wellbeing, as well as making you sharper and more focused.

They are also useful for helping you to manage your current stress levels or emotional triggers more effectively.

In order to increase your likelihood of participating in the programme, read and prepare for each practice the night before.

If you miss a day, you might want to practise the one you missed at the weekend. For most of the tools, each day builds on the previous one, so practicing them sequentially is preferable.

Be present when practicing.

CHAPTER TWO

The Breath

The mind is the king of the senses, and the breath is the king of the mind. [1]

Changing the way you breathe is one of the most powerful things you can do to impact your stress levels.

According to the American Institute of Stress, "Deep breathing increases the supply of oxygen to your brain and stimulates the parasympathetic nervous system, which promotes a state of calmness. Breathing techniques help you feel connected to your body – it brings your awareness away from the worries in your head and quiets your mind."[2]

When we are stressed, our breathing is affected. It tends to be shallow, which has the knock-on effect of making us even more stressed. It is a cycle that many people either aren't aware of or don't know how to break.

Practicing a few simple breathing techniques can enable you to break the cycle of your stress responses, calming the central nervous system and triggering parasympathetic stimulation.

Positions for the Breathing Practices

Many of the techniques can be carried out either in a sitting position or lying down. You want to make these exercises as accessible as possible in the office and in everyday life, so it is important not to be too rigid about them. At the same time, there are a few considerations for both the sitting and the lying down exercises that will maximise their effectiveness.

Sitting

If you are sitting, ensure that you are upright (without being too rigid). Slouching will hinder the practice.

Using the back of a dining chair with a pillow for comfort is a good way to ensure you remain upright.

Lying Down

Lying on your back has a number of benefits for your central nervous system. A traditional yoga practice usually ends with lying on the back in what is known as the Corpse Pose – it allows all the benefits of a yoga practice to be assimilated. This Corpse Pose, which brings a deep, meditative state of rest, can also be adapted to many everyday situations, regardless of whether you practice yoga or not. In Chapter 3 on the body, we will explore the Corpse Pose in more depth. In this chapter, our main focus is to use the pose in conjunction with breathing.

You can use it in conjunction with some of the breathing techniques as an emergency tool to relieve stress and exhaustion. The pose helps with sleep issues, as well as fatigue.

In addition, you can use it when you are already thriving, and want to accumulate more mental and physical energy and have a deep reset.

By the end of the four-week programme, you will be able to lie down in the Corpse Pose, decrease the rate of your breathing and slow your mind through meditation. Whilst lying on your back looks pretty easy, each of these stages is a skill that needs to be learnt and practised to get results, so we are looking for gradual and incremental improvements in each of these areas over the four weeks, rather than trying to achieve them all at once.

When you are lying down, do so on a semi-firm surface. Your bed is not the most suitable place for any of the breathing or relaxation postures, as lying in bed can induce a tendency to fall asleep (although you can use these postures in your bed at night if you are having problems with sleeping).

During the day, choose a semi-firm surface to ensure you stay awake, but not one that is so rigid that you can't get comfortable or relax.

Some people prefer to place supports such as a cushion or a rolled-up towel under their knees for support. This can also help the lower back to relax. If you are using a cushion for the neck, ensure that it is not too thick, as you want your airway to stay open: if your pillow is too thick, it will hamper this.

Covering the eyes is also an option when doing breathing or relaxation practices. It can help create a deepened state of relaxation.

Clothing

All the techniques in this book can be carried out in your regular work clothes in the office. However, if you are practicing them at night, loose, comfortable clothing is advised. Ensure that you are warm enough but not too hot. The optimum state is one of comfort and definitely not one of self-punishment.

Sunday Evening Preparation Practice - Focus on Your Breath

Time: 3 minutes

Purpose: To experience the effect that slowing the breath can have in a short space of time. To practise breathing into the abdomen.

1. Lie on your back in the Corpse Pose with your feet apart and your palms turned upwards. You can support your knees with a cushion and use a small pillow under your head.
2. Breathe in and out slowly, and softly, feeling the breath going in and out of your body. Notice your breath entering through your nose and follow its path into your lungs and back out again.
3. Now place your hands on your abdomen to see if you can feel your breath reaching your abdomen. If it is, you should feel your hands moving up and down. If you aren't able to feel your breath in your abdomen, we are going to learn a technique later this week that will enable you to do so.

Learning how to slow your breath will give you greater control over stressful or anxious situations. This alone can have a tremendously powerful effect on your emotions and wellbeing.

Monday – Releasing Tension from Your Body with Your Breath

As we highlighted earlier, slowing the breath can change the chemical reactions of your body. In this practice, as you combine the tensing and relaxing of your muscles or specific areas of your body with your breath, you can release even more tension.

Time: 1-3 minutes

Practice: At work or at home

Purpose: To be used when you are feeling physical tension or stress, any time of the day.

Practice: Breath and Body

1. Sit in a comfortable, upright position with your back supported.
2. Begin focusing on your breath. Breathe in deeply, pressing your feet into the ground. Breathe out, releasing your feet.
3. When you breathe in again, squeeze your knees and thighs together. As you breathe out, allow them to separate.
4. On your next in-breath, squeeze your buttocks together and simultaneously relax your belly. Slowly release your buttocks as you breathe out, keeping your belly relaxed.
5. Breathing in again, clench your hands into fists and press your arms into your sides. As you breathe out, relax and release.

6. Breathe in, lifting your shoulders upwards towards your ears. As you breathe out, release and relax them. (If you have a lot of shoulder tension you may want to repeat this step several times.)
7. This time as you breathe in, turn your head to the right. As you breathe out, turn your head to the centre. Then breathe in as you turn your head to the left and out as you turn your head to the centre. Repeat a further two times on each side.
8. Now breathe in, scrunch up your eyes and clench your teeth. Then breathe out and as you do so, relax your face.
9. Spend a few moments breathing slowly and noticing the effects on your body.

Repetition: Repeat this exercise frequently throughout the day today – perhaps each hour, or alternatively, before tea and lunch breaks.

Adaptation: You can adapt this practice to when you are standing in a queue or waiting for someone. You may want to omit turning your head (and scrunching up your eyes) if you are in a public place.

Tuesday – Chest Breathing and Abdominal Breathing

Many of us don't know how to breathe into our abdomens. This is largely because we haven't been taught how. There are primarily two types of breathing: chest breathing and abdominal or belly breathing.

When you chest breathe, the chest muscles inflate the lungs by pulling up the rib cage. The chest expands and contracts but the abdomen does not. Chest breathing does not deliver the full capacity of oxygen to the bloodstream.

When people hyperventilate, they are experiencing a very extreme version of chest breathing. Many of us chest breathe the majority, if not all, of the time.

When you belly breathe, your entire lung capacity is used. The diaphragm and the abdominal cavities are engaged; the lungs can fully inflate on the inhale, creating a greater flow of oxygen into the bloodstream, and on the exhale, they can expel a larger amount of carbon dioxide. It is therefore beneficial to learn how to belly breathe, and today's practice will enable you to do so.

Practice: Three-Part Breathing Exercise

Purpose: To enable you to determine the difference between breathing into the chest and breathing into the abdomen.

Practice time: 1-10 minutes

Practice: The main part of this technique is practised at home today so that you can spend some time identifying the difference between chest breathing and belly breathing.

Preparation

Sit or lie with your hands by your sides. Ensure your arms and legs are not crossed.

1. Begin breathing deeply, slowly and consistently.

2. Take your attention inside your body by following the breath as it moves in and out of your body. Notice the breath going in through your nose, expanding your chest and diaphragm, and moving your muscles as you breathe. Then follow it as it exits your body in the same way.

Three-Part Breathing

3. Place your flat palms on the top of your chest.

4. Breathe in and out, and as you do, feel your chest rising and falling. Repeat this three times, ensuring that you expel all the air from the chest in between each breath.

5. Now move your hands onto your ribs.

6. On an out-breath, place your fingertips on your ribs so that the middle fingers are touching each other.

7. Inhale deeply, and as you do, notice your middle fingers separating as your ribs expand.

8. Breathe out slowly until your middle fingers meet again. Repeat this three times.

9. Next, move your hands to your abdomen so that your middle fingers are in line with your navel. As you breathe in, feel your hands expanding upwards. As you breathe out, notice your hands dropping again. Repeat three times.

10. When you have completed the practice, continue sitting or lying as you breathe slowly and deeply for several breaths into the abdomen.

To extend this practice, continue breathing slowly and deeply for several minutes.

Adaptation: This technique is ideal for alleviating tension in the office. When you have practised it at home, use it any time you are stressed in the office. Take three long, deep slow breaths into the chest, then ribs, then abdomen, placing your hands on your body to guide you if you want.

Tip: Did you notice that tension in your physical body was preventing you from relaxing? Usually breathing releases tension, but if there was an accumulation of knots in your physical body, we are going to explore some different techniques that will help you release these in Chapter 3. In the meantime, if there is lots of tension in your body, you can practise doing this technique after physical exercise, particularly when you have stretched. This will enable you to have a deeper relaxation experience.

Wednesday – Walking and Breathing

Although a number of the breathing and mindfulness tools in this book are fairly static, you can also take them out and about with you. It is essential to learn the skills of breathing effectively while you are on the move; otherwise you can start to think of these techniques as something that you practise when you are in a room alone, rather than dynamic tools that can be used in the real world during everyday activities.

Time: 5 minutes

Purpose: To become more centred and present while walking.

Practice: Begin by practicing this technique outside.

Exercise: Walking and Breathing

Establish a deep breathing pattern as you are walking. Take four steps as you breathe in and seven steps as you breathe out.

Reminder: Count more steps on your out-breath because slowing down the out-breath triggers the parasympathetic nervous system.[3]

Check that your breathing is smooth and even. Although you are counting, it is important not to pause or hold the breath whilst you are counting. It should be one continuous breath in for four steps, followed by one continuous breath out for seven steps.

Ensure that you are walking, not marching. Softening the way your feet hit the ground will positively impact the central nervous system. Also, this practice will have less impact if you feel you are rushing. If you feel stressed when you start, intentionally slow the pace of your steps down for a more calming effect.

If you have been in your head or up in the air, this technique will help to ground you. To accelerate the grounding effect (and also to give your mind something to do during the practice), take your attention to the soles of your feet as you walk, and focus on each foot in turn as it touches the ground.

Once you have done this a number of times, you can increase to eight steps on the in-breath and twelve steps on the out-breath.

Adaptation: Once you have practiced this process out in the open, use it at any time of the day where you are walking, even if your journey is only a few moments long. Try it walking from the car park to your office, between meetings, on the way to bathroom breaks or walking to the cafeteria. (You will find that the benefits of using it for short times and often will outweigh the benefits of practicing it every now and again.)

Thursday – Lying on Your Front

It isn't only lying on your back that will enable you to relax. In fact, some people experience greater relaxation with the breathing techniques when they are lying on their front. As well as the immediate relaxation benefits, it is also said to induce better sleep, regularisation of blood pressure and reduce anxiety.

Practice: Crocodile Breathing

Time: 1-5 minutes

Practice: At home

Contraindication: Do not use during pregnancy.

1. Lie on your stomach, placing your legs a comfortable distance apart with toes pointing outwards.

2. Make your arms into right angles in front of you so that your fingers touch the inside of your elbow creases.
3. Rest your forehead on your crossed arms.
4. Breathe in through your nose and out through your mouth.
5. As you breathe in, you will feel your abdomen lift. As you breathe out, you will feel your abdomen pressing into the floor.
6. Continue in this position for five minutes.

Repetition: If you are comfortable doing this practice, use it regularly throughout the programme. It is recommended that you practise it daily. However, since we are introducing a series of different tools in this programme, I recommend that you intersperse it with some of the other breathing techniques in the programme so that you experience a variety of different exercises throughout the week.

Tip: Are you finding that your mental chatter is taking your focus off the practice? If so, try focusing your attention on the path of the breath as it moves around your body. This will give your mind something to do. It is likely that you will keep getting distracted at first, and the aim isn't 100 per cent focus, but rather noticing when you have gone into your thinking, and then coming back to following the breath. We will be giving you further tools to deal with your mental chatter in Chapter 4.

Friday – Clearing the Brain with the Breath

One breathing practice, which is sometimes described as "brain flossing" in yoga, can help you to clear your brain so you can think more effectively. We all know that flossing our teeth can help them to be cleaner, and this technique has a similar effect on the brain.

Time: 3-5 minutes

Purpose: To gain clarity of thought

Practice: You can do this sitting at your desk.

Exercise: Brain Flossing

1. Lean your right elbow on your desk. Hold your right hand with your palm facing you and place your first and middle finger between your eyebrows with your little finger curled down.
2. With your eyes closed, block your right nostril with your thumb and breathe in through your left nostril to the count of four. Remove your thumb and close your left nostril with your ring finger and breathe out through your right nostril for a count of seven.
3. Breathe in through the right nostril to the count of four, then close it with the thumb and breathe out of the left nostril to the count of seven.
4. Continue, breathing in through the left, out through the right, in through the right, out through the left counting four as you breathe in and seven as you breathe out.

5. After eight full rounds, remove your hand and take eight further breaths in and out of both nostrils counting four on the way in and seven on the way out.

Repetition: This technique can be used any time that you need to clear you mind. Try it several times throughout the day today and repeat it any time that your head becomes foggy during the programme.

Weekend Practice

Throughout the week, we have practised a series of tools that can also be adapted to the weekend. If the weather allows it this weekend, aim to practice the walking and breathing practice for an extended period of 10–20 minutes.

Also, see if you can make time to do one of the sitting or lying down techniques from the week. One suggestion would be to take the Corpse Pose lying on your back, and practise abdominal breathing again. When you find that you are expanding your lungs to the point where your abdomen is moving, you might try lying in this posture for 10 minutes with your eyes covered, in order to experience a deep rest. You can soften the breath once you have determined that you are breathing into your abdomen, as breathing too deeply can make you dizzy at first, particularly if you aren't used to getting so much oxygen into your bloodstream.

Summary of Chapter Two

Main Purpose of Breathing Practices:

- Deep breathing increases the supply of oxygen to your brain and stimulates the parasympathetic nervous system, which promotes a state of calmness.
- Breathing techniques help you feel connected to your body and quiet your mind.

Summary of Practices

Monday – Breath and Body

Used any time of the day, but this is particularly useful when you are feeling physical tension or stress.

Sitting upright with your back supported, focus on your breath. Breathe in, pushing your feet into the floor, breathe out releasing them. Follow the same pattern of creating tension on your in-breath and releasing on your out-breath for your knees and thighs. When you repeat for your buttocks, relax your belly as you squeeze your buttocks. Include clenching your hands into fists, and raising your shoulders. For your neck, coordinate your breathing with the movements of your head. Finish by scrunching your face up tightly on an in-breath and releasing it on an out-breath.

Tuesday – Three-Part Breathing Practice

Used to help you to breathe into your abdomen.

Lying or sitting, place your hands on your chest, feeling your chest rising and falling as you breathe. Then with your hands on your ribs, feel the middle fingers separate when you breathe in, and connect again when you breathe out. Next, with your hands on your abdomen and in line with your navel, feel your abdomen rising as you inhale and falling as you exhale (without forcing or straining).

Wednesday – Walking and Breathing

This enables you to become more present and relaxed as you walk. It is also a great exercise for helping you to ground yourself.

Establish a deep breathing pattern as you are walking. Start with breathing in for four steps and out for seven steps. Ultimately, you will be counting eight steps as you breathe in and twelve steps as you breathe out. Keep a smooth, even step and ensure your feet are landing softly. Take your attention into the soles of your feet to feel more grounded.

Thursday – Crocodile Breathing

Lying on your stomach with your toes pointing outwards, rest your forehead on your crossed arms. Breathing in, feel your belly lift, and breathing out, feel your belly contacting the floor.

Friday – Brain Flossing

With your right elbow on your desk, place your first and middle finger between your eyebrows and use your thumb and ring finger to alternatively block and unblock your nostrils. Breathe in for four on the left side and out for seven on the right. Then breathe in for four on the right and out for seven on the left. Repeat for several rounds and, removing your hand, finish with several breaths in and out.

Main Outcome of This Chapter:

This chapter is designed to help you develop a regular deep breathing practice. Ensure that you have several breathing tools that you can use in various situations and practise them regularly throughout the programme alongside the other techniques.

CHAPTER THREE

The Body

There is more wisdom in your body than in your deepest philosophy.

Friedrich Nietzsche

Your body is the vehicle through which you achieve your mission in life. It is also your centre for physical pleasure and feeling. Used effectively, and kept well-balanced, the body can both support you to accomplish your vision and goals, and enable you to experience a variety of sensory pleasures.

For many of us, our bodies are far from centred and balanced. Instead of listening to our bodies, we ignore the signs that they are sending out to us. We use caffeine to stimulate us to be able to achieve our daily goals, and we may even use alcohol or other drugs to help us switch off at the end of the day. Often these unhelpful habits are created because we are not aware of healthy alternatives, which this book provides.

Just as in the previous chapter where we helped you to change your relationship with your breath, in this chapter we are going to support you to change your relationship with your body.

In this chapter we are predominantly going to be focusing on how to release tension from your physical body. We've already highlighted the correlation between the body, the mind and the emotions, but it is worth reiterating that our negative thoughts create chemical reactions that increase adrenaline and other stress hormones in the body. By now, you have hopefully already experienced some changes in your body if you have been carrying out the breathing techniques each day, practicing mindfulness and meditation techniques, and stopping the negative chain of thoughts that inevitably create stress and tension in your body.

However, if you have noticed that physical tension is interfering with your meditation practice or draining your energy levels, then the tools that you learn this week will enable you to take more control over what is going on in your body.

Often, we learn patterns of tension and repeat them so frequently that they become normalised. The practices this week are going to enable you to interrupt these patterns, taking your body out of sympathetic nervous system stimulation and into the parasympathetic state of rest and repair.

Over the next five days we are going to work on a number of different levels. The first concerns how, when we place an intention to relax on our physical bodies with our minds, we can influence its state. The second is the link between the breath and the body. We have already touched upon this in the previous chapter, but in this chapter you will learn how to further tense and flex your muscles in combination with your breath, to achieve deeper relaxation. We will also explore movements which loosen the body, enabling you to release more tension.

Sunday Evening Preparation Practice

Time: 2 minutes

Sit in a quiet place and take your attention inside your body. Notice any areas of tension.

Monday – Releasing Tension When You Are Travelling To Work

Your journey to and from work can be a time when you accumulate a lot of tension. Unless you walk to work through a sunny country field or work from home, it is likely that your journey is littered with sound pollution, the stress of fellow travellers, delays, and other issues that cause you to accumulate physical and mental tension. Whether you cycle, walk, run, drive or take public transport to work, today we are going to look at your journey to and from work and identify any areas where you may be accumulating stress and tension.

Driving - Technique for Reducing Tension when in Traffic

If you drive to work, you are probably already aware that driving can cause tension, particularly if you get caught in traffic. Although you might not necessarily get caught in a traffic jam today, learn the following when you are sitting stationary in your car, for example, in the car park. You can then save it to help to relax your posture, create greater concentration and release physical tension when you do get stuck in traffic.

1. Loosen your hands on the steering wheel. Then breathe in and out. When you are breathing in, raise your shoulders towards your ears, and let them go on the out-breath. Then circle them backwards and forwards.
2. Lower your shoulders and at the same time, sit back and feel your back and your buttocks on the car seat,

and your feet on the pedals. Take several long, intentional breaths.
3. If necessary, repeat the shoulder exercises several times until your shoulders feel relaxed and you are more focused in the present moment.

Cycling

Although as a cyclist you probably won't get stuck in traffic, you may notice physical tension building in your body if you are late. Providing it is safe for you to do so and it doesn't distract you from the traffic around you, slightly release the grip you have on your handlebars and create some movement in your shoulders as you cycle. Also notice if you are in your head worrying about being late; if you are, then bring your focus fully back onto the task of cycling to work. Use the experience to see how present you can be, keeping your eyes on the road and becoming very aware of your physical body. This will also make for an even safer cycling experience because if you are stressed and fear focused, you are much less safe on the road than if you are present and vigilant.

Walking

If you walk to work, you can also encounter stress if you set out late, or if you have a high amount of pedestrian crossings or noisy traffic on your route. Notice any accumulation of physical tension in your body and deal with it as you walk. Shrug your shoulders to release tension while you are in motion or waiting at traffic lights. Practise deep breathing, slowing the out-breath and matching your breath to your steps as we did in Week

One, in order to give yourself something to focus on. Notice if you have left the present moment, and every time you find yourself in your head stressing about being late, take your attention to the soles of your feet and feel each foot as it makes contact with the pavement.

Also, expanding your focus far and wide can help you to feel calmer. You may notice that you have a very narrow focus when you walk, especially if you are stressed. Instead, create broader peripheral vision by expanding your visual focus far and wide, and notice the impact this has on your physiology.

One more consideration if you walk to work is whether your route is noisy and traffic polluted. If it is, you might want to minimise noise pollution with some gentle music. You may be used to the noise on one level, but it still has an effect on your central nervous system, making you more hypervigilant than a serene setting does. Minimising the impact can have a positive effect on the rest of your day and mean you arrive at work more refreshed.

Public Transport

If you take public transport to work, you need to take extra care, as you not only have your own stress levels to think of, but also those of your fellow travellers. In Chapter 5, we are going to give you tools to deal with others effectively, many of which you can employ when you are on your route to work. But for this week, become aware of the tension that mounts in your body when you are travelling.

Bring your shoulders towards your ears and release them several times as you sit in the bus or on the train. You can also circle them in each direction. Yawning will also help you release tension from your jaw. You may feel self-conscious about moving your body and stretching at first, but the choice is between having physical tension that might affect the rest of your day or risk being judged by outsiders.

If your route is quite noisy, you may want to accompany this with soft music.

Whatever your mode of travel to and from work, don't forget to tune into nature on your journey. For example, notice and appreciate the blue sky, that rose bush in somebody's front garden or that willow tree at the end of the road. Nature is one of the best stress busters and it's free.

Tuesday – Movements to Loosen the Body

The following exercises can be used to release tension from the body.

Time: 3-5 minutes

Purpose: To release physical tension from the body.

Practice: At work at your desk or in any other situation where you feel physical tension.

Contraindications: If you have neck or shoulder injuries, consult with your doctor or Health Care Provider before carrying out these techniques.

Loosening Exercises

Sit on an armless chair or stool, keep your back straight and start with your head and spine upright (but not rigid).

Hands:

Let your arms hang loosely between your knees or by your sides.

Shake your hands vigorously as though shaking off water.

Shoulders:

Imagine that someone is lifting you by the shoulders, and that they suddenly let go. Let your shoulders drop quickly.

Imagine you are holding a heavy weight in each hand, and your shoulders are being pulled down. Drop the weights and let your shoulders relax.

Roll your shoulders alternately, first forward six times, then backward six times.

Neck:

Allow your head to drop gently forward, whilst simultaneously imagining it is getting heavier. Then, pretend that someone has put a hand under your forehead, and raises it slowly back with no effort on your part.

Slowly and gently turn your head from side to side, trying to look behind you (without forcing or straining), three or four times each way.

Ankles:

Take off your shoes if you can and slowly rotate each ankle in turn, six or seven times in each direction.

Thighs:

Press your knees and thighs firmly together, then quickly release them, and allow your legs to flop apart.

Adaptation: You can repeat these practices throughout the day. If you have one particular body part that gets tight, such as your shoulders, you may want to focus on the process for that body part each hour. Set an alarm to remind you to practise each hour today and notice the effect it has on your energy levels by the end of the day. After today, incorporate this into your daily routine, particularly if you have a lot of physical tension.

Wednesday - The Corpse Pose

We began exploring the Corpse Pose, where you incorporated deep relaxation whilst lying on your back and accompanied this with breathing techniques. In this chapter we will deepen this exploration.

You may have noticed that tension in your mind or physical body was preventing you from carrying out the practices effectively, so in this session, we will combine tensing and releasing your muscles with deep breathing. In addition, we will use the mind to focus on each body part individually, making this a technique that incorporates all the elements we have learnt so far.

Corpse Pose

Time: 10-20 minutes

Purpose: To rejuvenate the body, release tension, focus thinking. Total body reset.

Practice: At home in the evening, particularly at the end of a long stressful day, or any time you want rejuvenation. If you work from home, practicing this around 3.00 pm for 10-20 minutes can leave you refreshed and rejuvenated for the remainder of the working day, and is a much better substitute than coffee.

Corpse Pose – With Tension and Relaxation Exercises

1. Set a soft alarm for 10-20 minutes. Lie on your back on a comfortable surface (preferably other than your bed) with your eyes covered if you prefer. Have your palms face up and a little bit away from your body, and your feet hip distance apart. For extra comfort, place a small cushion under your neck and another cushion or bolster under your knees so your back is supported.
2. Take your mental focus to each body part as you move up your body. Tense each body part on the in-breath. Keep each body part tensed for several seconds, releasing on the out-breath. Start at your feet and work your way up, as follows:

    (a) Feet and calves – tensing both at once and release.
    (b) Thighs – as above.
    (c) Buttocks – as above.
    (d) Lower back – as long as you don't have any back problems, very gently tense or arch your lower

back and then release it. Take extreme caution when carrying out this part of the process and ensure that you do not jar your back in any way. If in doubt, miss this part out.

(e) Fists – clench both fists tightly and release.

(f) Arms and shoulders – tense your arms as you shrug your shoulders towards your ears and release.

(g) Upper back – *very gently* arch your upper back away from the floor, pushing your chest up and then letting it connect back with the floor again.

(h) Neck – don't tense your neck. Instead, very gently and slowly roll it to the left, back to the centre, and to the right, coordinating this with your breathing.

(i) Face – scrunch up your face and let it go.

3. Then take five deep, long, slow, audible breaths in and out. On this round of breathing you should be able to hear the breath in the back of your throat.

4. Take a further five deep breaths, slowing the out-breath even further. (Your breath does not need to be audible for this round.)

5. Take a further five deep breaths slowing the in- and out-breaths (but still ensuring the out-breath is longer than the in-breath).

6. Continue breathing in and out slowly and softly and by this point, inaudibly, until the alarm sounds. See how much you can slow your breath down during this practice (without forcing or straining). You can also pause a beat or two between each breath.

Tip: Whether you enjoyed the Corpse Pose and experienced a deep sense of relaxation, or found it challenging, you might want to try a yoga class to expand your experience. If you are feeling depleted, yoga can help you experience more energy. There are also more athletic types of yoga, some of which take place in a heated studio. These are good for you if you are pretty athletic and feel like you could benefit from a deep stretch (many of the more intense forms of yoga are less about breathing and relaxation and more about stretching the body). If you are feeling adventurous this week, search for and find a class in your area or look online for some resources.

Thursday – Relaxation with Intention

Just focusing on your physical body with intention can enable it to relax. This technique will enable you to experience how much your mind is connected with your body, and how you can influence your physical state simply by giving a command. This can be done sitting on the train or standing in a queue.

Time: 2-3 minutes

Purpose: To use the mind and intention to affect the state of the body.

1. Standing, sitting or lying down, slowly scan your body, giving each muscle the command to relax three times. Start at your feet and work your way up to the top of your head. Repeat the following commands silently three times for each body part (ensure that you are

repeating the commands firmly yet gently, rather than aggressively):

(a) Right foot relax, right calf relax, right thigh relax, right buttock relax.
(b) Left foot relax, left calf relax, left thigh relax, left buttock relax.
(c) Belly relax.
(d) Lower back relax, upper back relax.
(e) Right hand relax, right forearm relax, right upper arm relax, right shoulder relax.
(f) Left hand relax, left forearm relax, left upper arm relax, left shoulder relax.
(g) Throat relax, neck relax, head relax, face relax.

Adaptation: Sitting at your desk or in a meeting: if you notice tension in any particular body part, deepen your breath and command the body part that is tense to relax.

Tip: If you have been drinking lots of caffeine, it is probably no surprise to you that it could be impacting your stress levels. A study by researchers at Duke University Medical Center shows that caffeine taken in the morning has effects on the body that persist until bedtime and it amplifies stress consistently throughout the day.[4] Reducing or eliminating caffeine can go a long way to reducing your stress levels and will complement the tools found in this programme. It is difficult to try to relax on a caffeine high, as it stimulates the brain and the nervous system, creating the opposite effect of relaxation. (If you want, you can cut down your caffeine intake gradually, e.g. from 4 to 3 cups a day for a week, then to 2, etc.)

Friday – Pattern Interrupt

One of the greatest challenges we face with our physical body is the patterns that we have fallen into. In Chapter 4 on the mind we are going to explore how, when we repeat a thought over and over again, neural connections are formed. Something similar happens with our bodies, particularly if we have a routine that involves going to work at a similar time every day: our bodies can start falling into certain patterns. These include things like feeling sluggish in the morning, dipping in energy around 3.00 pm, and feeling tired when we return home. We often assume that these patterns are just the way we are, but throughout this book, I explore with you ways of breaking limiting beliefs that you have about yourself and doing things differently.

If you have been falling into certain patterns with your body, simply try interrupting them. Personal Development Guru Anthony Robbins has spoken much about pattern interrupting, and catching yourself when you start to dip in energy. For today, apply some of the following suggestions, and then incorporate them into your daily routine if you find they help. Remember, you have repeated a number of your patterns over and over again, so it might take more than one intervention to break them.

Practice One: Get Up Frequently

We weren't built to sit at a desk all day. But if that is part of your job, ensure that you get up frequently so that your energy doesn't become sluggish.

Practice Two: Step Outside

Step outside if you can, or at least stick your head out of the window. If you can get to the park or a green area at lunchtime (and it's warm enough), take your shoes and socks off and put your bare feet on the earth. Put your mobile or other technical devices a short distance away from you while you do this so that you can fully recharge. Some people use this practice, called Earthing, for twenty minutes a day, and report dramatic increases in their health and wellbeing.[5]

Practice Three: Change Your Pace

Walk somewhere with the intention of shifting your internal climate. If you are sluggish, make it a brisk walk. If your mind is racing, make it a slow, intentional walk.

Practice Four: Make Some Noise

If you can go somewhere private for a minute or two, such as the file room or a storage room, use the opportunity to make some noise! Clapping and stamping can have an immediate effect on your energetic state, jolting you out of your current pattern.

Practice Five: Bounce

If you work from home, buy a mini trampoline for your office. According to research from NASA[6], rebounding is one of the most effective forms of exercise available. Jumping on a mini trampoline for fifteen minutes each day can strengthen cells, increase the flow of lymph in the body impacting immunity, improve cardiovascular health, as well as improving muscles, balance, coordination and flexibility. In addition, it is a great way to charge up your physical energy when you are flagging.

If you have your own office at work, you can install a mini trampoline. Alternatively, try having one at home and using it when you come home from work and need to burn off any excess stress. Accompanied by your favourite music, it can be a great stress buster.

Weekend Practices

This weekend, see if you can get a deeper appreciation of the connection between the breath, the mind and the body. If you have had a challenging week, spend time rejuvenating in the Corpse Pose and tensing and relaxing your muscles in coordination with your breath.

If you are more energised and going out and about this weekend, deepen your experience of walking meditation, matching your pace with your breath. Extend your walking meditation to noticing the space in between things. If you notice any tension in your body, pause and use some of the loosening exercises to shake it out.

At this stage we are looking for a dynamic interplay between the tools for breath, mind and body, so use this weekend to notice the relationship between them more, even if it is just for five or ten minutes.

Summary of Chapter Three

The main aim of this chapter is to enable you to:

- Use the journey to and from work to de-stress.
- Release tension, taking your body out of the stress of sympathetic nervous system stimulation and into the parasympathetic state of rest and repair.
- Place your intention on certain body parts, enabling them to relax.
- Flex and tense your muscles in combination with your breathing, enabling you to achieve deeper relaxation.

Summary of Practices

Monday – Releasing Tension When You Are Travelling To Work

If you drive to work, loosen your hands on the steering wheel when stuck in traffic. Lift shoulders up and down and then circle them. Include taking your intention inside your body and noticing your thought patterns.

Similar exercises can be carried out on a cycle, public transport or walking, with the emphasis on releasing tension from the shoulders, checking the thought patterns, and practicing being present whatever the situation.

Engage with nature from your car, the train window or as you are walking.

Tuesday – Loosening Exercises

Sit on an armless chair or stool. Shake your hands vigorously. Imagine that someone is lifting you by the shoulders, and that they suddenly let go. Let your shoulders drop quickly. Roll your shoulders backwards and forwards. Drop your head gently forward and imagine a hand lifting your forehead. Circle your ankles with your shoes off. Press your thighs together and then release them.

Wednesday - The Corpse Pose – With Tension and Relaxation Exercises

Lie on your back on a comfortable surface with your palms face up. You can support your knees and neck with a cushion, and cover your eyes too if you prefer. On an inhale, tense the following muscles, holding them for a few seconds and then relaxing on an exhale: feet, calves, thighs, buttocks, lower back, fists, arms and shoulders, upper back. Turn your neck slowly from side to side, coordinating with your breath. Scrunch up your face and let it go.

Then take five deep, long, slow, audible breaths in and out. On the following round, slow the out-breath and on the round after that slow the in- and out-breaths. Continue breathing slowly and softly.

Thursday – Relaxation with Intention

Focusing on your physical body with intention can enable it to relax. Scan your body from toe to head, pausing at each muscle point and giving it the command to relax three times.

Friday – Pattern Interrupt – Five Practices

Get up frequently, step outside, change your pace, make some noise or bounce. All these exercises will change your energy state when you need to shift up or down a gear.

Main Outcome of This Chapter:

Use body practices throughout the day to change and manage your energy state.

CHAPTER FOUR

The Mind

A man is what he thinks about all day long.
Ralph Waldo Emerson

One of the most effective things you can do in work and in life is to be here in this present moment. You have probably noticed that this is easier said than done.

Many of us don't actually know how to be present. You were probably not taught this at school, where much of the emphasis took you to a future moment of exam results, university and careers. You were probably not taught this at home either, with many of us being given the model of how to either dwell on the past or feel stressed or fearful about the future by our parents or caregivers.

There are four main ways you can fail to be present in the moment.

1. Dwell on the past and regret something that happened before
2. Dwell on the past and wish that things today were as good as they were then
3. Focus on the future whilst fearing what might happen
4. Believe a future moment will be better than this one.

If you are doing any of the above, it takes you away from being here, now.

There are a multitude of reasons why you are less effective when you aren't present. Each of the four ways that you leave the present moment can have a profound effect on the way you operate in both the working environment and your life in general. If you are dwelling on the past, believing that the times that went before were better, or longing for a future moment that is better than this one, it can leave you with a feeling of emptiness, longing or a lack of fulfilment. The language of this is usually something like "It was better when," or "It will be better when."

"It was better when" is something you will often hear in old people's homes where the residents might sit around talking about how life was better in times gone by. But you may also find yourself doing this in companies or organisations, talking about a 'golden era' of business and wishing you could get it back.

"It will be better when" is often the belief that guides many of our workplace interactions. We are constantly striving to make things better and to improve our situation. It's a naturally human response to want to grow, expand, evolve and create. It becomes problematic, however, when we postpone our happiness until we have achieved our goal. This is a challenge when you are constantly goal-orientated and the last goal gets replaced by the next one. If you are postponing your happiness until your goals are reached and constantly moving the goal posts, your life can feel empty and meaningless. It's not that you need to stop setting goals, but rather learn how to be present whilst continually reaching targets.

As we highlighted previously, other ways that you keep yourself from being in the moment are regretting something that went before and fearing something that might happen later. The language of these is "I wish this hadn't happened," or "What if this happens?" In both cases, stress is often triggered, making it harder for you to focus in the moment.

Many of us do both of these simultaneously without realising that we are doing them. The result is that part of us is here now, whilst the other part is jumping into the past, remembering something that didn't go well and taking it into the future as evidence of why something is likely to fail.

Imagine, for example, that you have a huge deal on the table. Instead of feeling excited, you start to feel a sense of dread. You go into your mind, telling yourself the story of the deal that went to your competitor two years ago. Other perceived failures start to pop into your head. Then you jump forward into the future, imagining that this deal will also fail. If you are really spiralling, you might even find yourself picturing how it will lead to you losing everything. You picture your house being repossessed, with a series of dramatic scenes unfolding in your mind, accompanied by a deepening sense of dread. If it is really dramatic, you might end up with a picture of you homeless and begging on the streets!

Often people say that the imagined future failures flashed by in their mind so quickly that they barely even noticed they were there. Fast or slow, they still have an impact on how we feel and act in the present. They trigger a series of chemical responses that are present when we go and make the deal. If we are lucky, we 'pull it off' or 'get away with it'. But if the effects of the triggering are more visible on the outside, it might create problems. The signs of stress might be perceived by associates as a lack of confidence and could impact the outcome of the deal.

Mastering present moment awareness impacts every area of our life, and the results of being present are often visible to others.

Using Your Mind

Used properly, your mind is a tool to help you create a vision and purpose for your life and support you to fulfil it.

However, many of us haven't sharpened our mind to the point that it fully supports our mission and purpose in life. We may have a clear idea of what we want to achieve, but find that our mind, far from supporting our goals, can hinder or conflict with them. You may at times find yourself living divided, as you have a clear idea of what you want and a mind that seems to contradict your goals.

When we are worrying, obsessing and doubting, it can feel like we don't have a choice in these behaviours. They are often patterns we learnt from those around us, which become normalised. In his book *Thunk!*, Sandy Newbigging highlights:

If you cannot switch off and stop thinking at will, then your relationship with your mind has become unbalanced and unproductive. Rather than using your mind as the magnificent tool that it is, and then putting it down when you're done, your mind is quite literally using you! As a result of incessant thinking, I would suggest that you aren't actually thinking anymore, but instead, you are being thunk![7]

Fortunately, if these are familiar patterns, they are ones you have learnt, so you can unlearn them too. This chapter will give you tools that, if practised frequently, will enable you to choose how to use your mind so it is no longer 'thinking you'.

You want to be able to use your mind more as you would any other tool – when you want to solve a problem, create or build something – and then put it down when you are done.

The practices that are presented in this book aren't designed to stop these thoughts altogether, but rather to change your relationship with your mind. In his book *Mind Calm,* Sandy Newbigging states that meditation and mindfulness practices aren't about stopping the thoughts, but rather changing our relationship to them. He explains that we need to be seeking peace *with* mind rather than peace *of* mind. This is a crucial distinction because many meditation and mindfulness practices mislead us into believing that we need to stop our thoughts to experience peace. Instead, we need to change our relationship with our thoughts so that they do not have the negative impact on us.

There have been varying reports that we have between 50,000 – 70,000 thoughts a day, although there seems to be some disparity about what the actual number is. Most of them go unnoticed, but others trigger an emotional response from us. They are usually created from our life experiences, particularly the ones that have been more traumatic. We learnt to hold and reference what went before and that is why they are often accompanied by an emotional response such as fear, shame, anger, self-doubt and so on.

The practices this week are designed to help you change your relationship with your thoughts. Although our focus for this spans a week, it will most likely take more than seven days to change your relationship with your mental climate; some people spend years or even decades exploring tools and processes similar to those in this chapter. This week will give you an excellent grounding in these practices, increasing your awareness of your thoughts and emotions, and giving you tools to interrupt existing patterns so that you can begin to transform them. The tools in this week's practice fall into four categories.

Firstly, you'll be asked to observe your thoughts and the impact they are having on your physical and emotional wellbeing.

Secondly, you'll be given tools to enable you to interrupt destructive thought processes.

Thirdly, you'll be introduced to meditation and mindfulness practices that will enable you to be more present and conscious throughout your daily life, both at home and in the workplace.

Finally, you'll be given tools and processes that will enable you to adopt more positive thought processes. By the end of the week you will be able to notice when you are triggered by your thoughts and halt your old patterns before they spiral into hours, days or even weeks of negative thinking.

Sunday Evening Preparation Practice

Technique: Set a timer for one minute and then count how many thoughts you have.

Remember – your thoughts are often so familiar that you might not even recognise them as thoughts. Some people do this exercise and say they haven't had any thoughts, but when I press the point, they often say they had the thought "I'm not thinking anything," which is still a thought!

The point of this technique is not to analyse your thoughts, but rather to enable you to become aware of how many thoughts you are having. During this following week, our aim is not to reduce or stop thoughts, but rather to change how you relate to them.

<u>Monday</u> – Noticing When You Are Being Dragged Along by Your Thoughts

Have you noticed what happens when you get on a thought train? It's literally like you are being pulled along and at the same time you either don't know that you have a choice to get off the train, or you don't know how to get off.

In *Thunk!,* Sandy Newbigging describes this as the red car.[8] He outlines a scene where you and your friends are sitting at the side of a road watching the cars go by, when suddenly, you grip onto the bumper of the red car that is passing. You are getting dragged along by the red car and at the same time you are screaming, "This red car is hurting me!" Actually, it isn't the red car that is hurting you, but rather the fact that you are holding onto it.

The same thing happens in the mind with our thoughts. It is never the thought itself that is hurting you, but the fact that you are holding onto it. As we've already highlighted, at least 50,000 thoughts are going to pass through your mind every day. Most of them are like the other cars passing. But then a thought will come that has some significance or relevance to you and you will start to dwell on it. And often when a thought comes that is significant, it is also accompanied by a feeling or emotion. You feel something and that feeling makes the thought even more real.

Technique - Notice Your Red Cars

The best time to practise this is when you are not triggered by your thoughts. Then, you can easily observe the ones that have more of a pull.

This exercise is actually most useful when you are triggered by a thought.

Time: 1 minute

Purpose: To notice when you are being dragged along by your thoughts and to intervene.

Usage: Any time you catch yourself thinking about something that is bothering you, particularly if there is a stressful emotion attached to the thought.

The Thought: Notice the thoughts that have a tendency to drag you along.

The Emotion: At the same time, become aware of what happens in your body when you are experiencing one of these thoughts. Because we focused on the body last week, it is probably easier for you to locate where it is showing up in your body.

Awareness: Sometimes placing your awareness on the thought is enough. Most of the time we get dragged along by the red car without even realising it is happening, particularly because the emotion that accompanies it makes it feel even more real. Watch the thought and its impact upon you. Sit with it for a few minutes. Can you separate the thought from the feeling, or at least notice the difference between the thought you are having and the feeling it is creating?

Breathing: If there is still a strong feeling associated with the thought after you have watched it for a few moments, practise breathing into where you feel the thought is in your body. Focus on the thought. Slow your breath down, breathing in for four and out for seven. You should experience some kind of cognitive shift or realisation that it is just a thought and it is not real.

Variation: Many people who have tried this practice relate more to the metaphor of a train than a car. If you don't relate to the image of being dragged along by a car, it can help to see yourself as having got onto a train of thought. You have the power to stop the train and get off. Awareness usually stops the train and the breathing practice can help you to get off.

It is worth noting that you may not always immediately notice when you are being dragged along by your thoughts, particularly if you have been rehearsing different thought patterns over and over again. In *It's The Thought That Counts*, former pharmaceutical scientist Dr David Hamilton highlights that when we repeat a particular thought pattern, it creates neural connections in our brain. Recent research on brain plasticity indicates that we can undo old neural connections and form new ones. But we often need to repeat new patterns before the new connections become stabilised, which is why you might find that you have to interrupt your thoughts and break their patterns numerous times before you get results.

Think of it like a book. At first you might get half way through the book before you realise you have been obsessively or destructively thinking. You catch yourself, but instead of judging yourself, you just notice, "Oh, I was on that train of thought again." You might even congratulate yourself for noticing the pattern. Next time, you get to chapter three before you break the pattern. Following that, you break the pattern before the end of the first chapter. With more practice, you find yourself breaking the pattern when you are on the first page. Then, before you know it, you are simultaneously getting on a train of thought and stopping yourself before the train leaves the station. You don't even make it past the first paragraph before you think, "Hold on, I've been down that track before." So, halting your thoughts before they spiral out of control is definitely a process, but one that is worth the dedication and effort so that your mind is no longer thinking you.

Tuesday – Becoming More Mindful

Now that you have a tool to interrupt the pattern of your thoughts, over the next few days we will be sharing some tools that will enable you to experience more mindfulness.

The dictionary defines mindfulness as "the quality or state of being conscious or aware of something." It is also defined as "a mental state achieved by focusing one's awareness on the present moment, while calmly acknowledging and accepting one's feelings, thoughts, and bodily sensations."

Mindfulness practices help you focus on the here and now, taking your mind off future fears or past regrets. Whilst practicing mindfulness, even if your mind does stray into worrying or obsessing, the objective is to bring yourself back to the present moment without judging yourself for the fact that you left it.

Mindfulness has become a buzzword in the corporate world and in Chapter 6 we explore the research to support why so many companies and organisations are incorporating it into their strategic plans to increase productivity and employee happiness. Simply put, leaving the present moment to focus on our fears and concerns about the past and future is counterproductive to our health, happiness and creativity. The more present you can be, the sharper your mind will be.

Although there are countless mindfulness techniques available, over the next two days we will focus on two: one you can practise with your eyes open, and one you can practice with your eyes closed. Whilst there are numerous techniques in this programme, I strongly suggest that you develop a regular mindfulness practice using one or both of the following methods.

Practice: Notice The Space in Between Things

One technique is to notice the space in between things. There is a difference between the content and context of what is around us.

We are very content focused. If you look around the room you will notice all the things that are in the room. If I ask you what is surrounding you, you will no doubt name things like the desk, your chair, your computer, and so on. This is the content of your surrounding space. Most of us don't notice the context of those objects. The context is the space between everything that exists.

When we focus in on a specific object, it can often feel like our mind is getting tighter. Practise focusing in on one object now and you will see what I mean. It can feel like your eyes are scrunching up and your brain becomes tense.

When we do the opposite – focusing on the context of the objects that surround us – something changes in our brain. It feels like we are expanding mentally. Try it briefly before we go into the practice. Focus on a single object and then shift your focus on the space in between you and the object. Even practicing this technique for a brief moment can give your mind the space it needs to solve a problem or see things from a different perspective.

Purpose: To take you out of your head and enable you to return to present moment awareness.

Time: 1-10 minutes

Practice: At work or in any other situation. When you are too much in your head or your focus is too 'tight'. When you want to expand your thinking and make it more creative.

Start by noticing the objects in the room. Look around the room and mentally name five or six objects. If you have been in your head and not in your body, then the first part of the exercise can help to bring you back to the room.

1. Next, notice your body. If you are sitting, what are you sitting on? Can you feel your back against your chair and your behind on the seat? If you are standing, notice your feet on the floor.

2. Start to pay attention to your breath coming in and out of your body. Slow the breath down a little and breathe more consciously.

3. Now, return to the objects, but as you do, start defocusing your eyes on specific objects and become more aware of the space in between the objects. It's almost as if you let the objects go, and instead, put all your focus on the space that you are in.

4. Continue for 1–10 minutes.

5. Notice your mental state after this practice. It often brings about a state of calm and peace.

Deepening This Practice

You can continue this technique for several minutes, and instead of trying to keep all your awareness on the space in between things, move slowly between focusing on what your body is touching, focusing on your breath, and focusing on the space.

Adaptation One – Notice the Space In Between Things During a Meeting

This technique is a great one when you are in a meeting or presentation, particularly if you have the opportunity to be silent for a moment or two. If there is a lot of conflict in the meeting or you need to be able to think on your feet, take a few moments to notice the space in between things. If you have been practicing this regularly outside of a meeting situation, it can help to bring you instantly back to the present.

Adaptation Two – Taking Your Awareness Inside of You

Once you notice the context rather than the objects, close your eyes and take the experience internally for a few minutes. You will probably find this is very different to closing your eyes 'normally'. Often when we close our eyes, our attention stays in our brains and focuses on all the things we need to do or should have done. If you start by noticing the space in between things and then close your eyes, you will probably find that your attention is in your "wider" body instead. This is a great preparation for tomorrow's practice when you are going to learn a mindfulness meditation technique that you can carry out with your eyes closed.

Wednesday – Learning Mindfulness Meditation with Eyes Closed

In today's practice we are going to touch on our first formal meditation technique of the programme. Meditation can be carried out in any position, although sitting upright is preferable and also means you are less likely to fall asleep. In this programme we are moving away from a number of stereotypes that have grown around meditation, and encouraging you to take your meditation practice into the office and make time for it for short periods during the day. Also, as we established in Chapter 1, it is beneficial to develop a daily practice at home for a minimum of twenty minutes per day. There is a plethora of meditation techniques that you can use. Today you will learn a simple one, and you will also find further suggestions at the end of this chapter for you to try on the weekend.

Some tips for preparing your meditation space

- Some people find showering before meditation helps them to feel clearer and more focused during the process. This obviously does not apply if you are at work.
- You can meditate anywhere and at any time, but it helps to build in a regular time at a similar time each day for your 20-minute session. First thing in the morning or last thing at night is preferable. If you are

going to practise last thing at night, ensure that you don't wait until you are almost falling asleep.
- Ensure that you are not going to be distracted during the 20-minute session. Do what you can to limit outside noise.
- It is preferable not to meditate on a full stomach. If you have just eaten a heavy meal, your body is working to digest it and this can interfere with the flow of energy during meditation.
- Soft lighting, such as candlelight, is more effective than bright light.
- You may have seen more traditional meditation practices where the participant sits in a cross-legged position, known as the lotus position. Only attempt this if it is comfortable for you. This position can be adapted by placing a firm cushion on the floor near a wall to sit on, and another cushion behind you to support your back. If you require additional support, place a cushion under each knee and a blanket on the floor for your feet and ankles. It is essential that you don't do anything that makes you uncomfortable, because the discomfort will be a distraction from the practice and will prevent you from wanting to practise further.

Things that might occur while you are meditating

Falling asleep: This is a common one, particularly if you aren't getting enough sleep. It can be minimised by creating a comfortable upright position and choosing to carry out the practice when you aren't too tired.

A release of emotions: Hectic lifestyles can be used to distract us from our emotions. Sometimes when sitting still and taking our attention within, we are faced with emotions that we haven't dealt with. Unexpressed emotions can lead to all manner of physical and mental imbalances, so it is key that if you do experience an emotional response during meditation, you just let it be. There may be a tendency to try and push it down or even to stop the meditation because you don't want to feel a certain way. In that case, just remember that the meditation practice is only bringing to the surface what is already within you, and it is definitely better out than in. Seek professional help from a therapist if the practice brings up repressed memories or triggers severe emotional responses.

Insights: One of the reasons that many executives and thought leaders use meditation is that it can enable them to have insights that they would not otherwise have in an everyday state. Whilst insights are a valuable part of meditation, it is vital not to become too attached to them during the practice. If you have an insight and then spend the next twenty minutes planning how you are going to bring it into fruition in your work or your life, it will take you out of the meditative state and back into thinking mode. What you want to avoid is allowing your meditation time to become a planning meeting in your head! Instead, notice if you have an insight, go back to the meditation practice, and act on it after the session. This way you can give your practice the respect that it deserves.

Tranquillity and Bliss: Neuroscientist Candace Pert, who discovered the opiate receptor in the brain, is famous for repeatedly saying that "We are hard-wired for bliss." In other words, bliss is our natural state. What keeps us from this state primarily is our constant focus on what went before and what might come next. When we leave the present moment to obsess about the past or worry about the future, we take ourselves out of our state of bliss. If you think of the emotions as having a scale, with depression and fear at the bottom, and bliss and joy at the top, we cannot simultaneously be in a state of joy whilst being in a state of fear. When we meditate, and we return to the present moment, our fear centres are no longer triggered. For this reason, you might find yourself experiencing bliss and tranquillity at the same time as being present.

Self-judgement: There will be part of you that wants to assess or judge the meditation practice. You might find yourself having thoughts such as "Today's practice wasn't as good as yesterday's," or vice versa. Try to keep your judgements out of your meditation practice. If you are highly competitive, goal-driven and results-orientated, let this be the one place where you give yourself a break. It is a time to just be present with what is happening, without trying to control it or force it. This is the key to having an effective practice. You will probably also find that if you practise non-judgement within meditation, any old patterns of self-judgement you have in your life in general will begin to dissipate.

Practice: Mindfulness Meditation

Time: 10-20 minutes

Practice: For your first closed-eye mindfulness meditation it is recommended that you sit in a comfortable position where there are no distractions and disturbance from noise is limited. As you become more proficient in this technique, you can practise it any time you want to return to the present moment.

1. Set a soft alarm for the duration of the exercise. A minimum of 10 minutes is recommended, although as you have more experience with this technique, you can extend it to 20 or even 30 minutes.
2. Sit in a comfortable position with your eyes closed. This can either be a more traditional meditative posture or sitting upright on a chair with your back supported.
3. Take your awareness to your breath, observing it as it moves in and out.
4. There is no need to alter your breath or forcibly slow it down. However, as you observe your breath, you may notice that it changes on its own. Perhaps the speed, pace or depth alters naturally. Sometimes it may even feel like it pauses from time to time. Whatever happens with your breath, simply observe it.
5. If your attention drifts away from your breath and goes to a thought in your mind, a sensation in your body, or a sound in the environment, gently bring your awareness back to your breathing.

6. The key to carrying out this practice effectively is to relinquish any expectations you may have about its process. If you find yourself anticipating a particular experience, treat this as you would any other thought and gently bring your awareness back to your breath.
7. Continue until your alarm sounds, then take your attention off your breathing and sit in silence for a minute or two before slowly opening your eyes.

Thursday – Your Relationship with your Mind

As you develop tools and practices that support you to live more in the present moment, you may begin to notice times when your relationship with your mind is not so supportive. One of the most obvious ways you can spot if you have an unhealthy relationship with your mind is through your self-talk.

The point with your self-talk is that you have probably been talking to yourself in a similar voice throughout your life. It is often a voice that we learn in childhood, and if we experienced a lot of criticism from our primary caregivers or teachers, we often take their voice on as if it were our own. Not only that, but our self-talk becomes so familiar to us that we think it *is* us. Many people don't even consider that they can change their self-talk, let alone appreciating the impact this change would have on their self-esteem and sense of wellbeing.

For high achievers, self-talk tends to be critical when things don't go to plan. If there are any times when you have caught yourself calling yourself an idiot (or something stronger), you will know what I mean. But oftentimes, the insidious self-talk that I am referring to is subtler than name-calling. It is a barely audible background commentary about a lack of self-worth, and I have helped even the most successful individuals uncover it in themselves, often to their surprise.

Your self-talk can be summed up in the story you have about yourself based on your life experiences, and how you filter that story to judge yourself in the present day.

The key antidote to negative self-talk is awareness. The more aware you are of your self-talk, the better the chance you have of reframing it. Becoming aware of any stories you are telling yourself and stopping them in their tracks, as opposed to letting them run, is a key component to working with your self-talk.

Practice Part One – Awareness

Time: the whole waking day

For the duration of today, place your awareness on the quality of your self-talk. Aim to catch yourself in any judging or self-critical thoughts. Ensure that when you do, you avoid further judgement or analysis. Instead of asking, "Why am I so hard on myself?" which is another more subtle form of negative self-talk, simply observe yourself in these old, familiar patterns.

Practice Part Two – Ask Yourself Better Questions

Awareness might be enough to break the pattern of negative self-talk, but if you need extra help, change the quality of the questions you are asking yourself. Often negative self-talk comes in the form of questions such as "Why does this always happen to me?", "Why am I so depressed?" or "Why am I so stupid?" Questions such as these contain conclusions about your current state and lock you into more of the same situations. You can change the questions into something like, "What can I learn from this?" or "What needs to happen so I can do things differently?" or "What do I need to do to give me more energy?" and so on. These are open-ended questions that you might not have the answer to right away, but asking them creates more possibility. In my experience, staying with the open-ended questions means that answers to them will emerge at some point.

Similarly, if you make conclusions about yourself such as "I always get it wrong," "I'm no fun to be around," and so on, you can turn these into open, positive questions such as, "What do I need to do here?" or "What needs to happen for me to have more fun?"

Any time you catch yourself making a negative statement or asking a closed or conclusion-based question about yourself, switch it to a question that will enable you to move beyond the limitations or towards a solution.

Friday –Visualisation

At the start of this chapter, we highlighted how your mind is a powerful tool that often gets misused, and we have followed that up by giving you a number of tools to experience more presence and awareness. There is an additional practice that you can use regularly to sharpen the power of your mind, and that is visualisation.

Visualisation has a lot to do with the neural pathways in your brain. Over the past decade there has been more and more research that gives evidence of the brain's neuroplasticity or, in other words, its ability to change due to experience. The brain's physical structure and function can literally change and two of the ways you can influence it is with your thoughts and with visualisation. In *The Biology of Belief*, Stanford-trained cell biologist Bruce Lipton highlights how new connections between neurons can be formed, and that neurons can even be generated. This understanding has only come to the forefront in recent years, at least in the West. Prior to the release of this research, it was believed that our brains were set in our early years and couldn't be changed, hence the old proverb "You can't teach an old dog new tricks." Today we know: It may take a bit of time but you *can* teach an old dog new tricks!

Visualisation is a tool that can be used in a variety of situations. If you are fearful that you can't achieve something, you will probably find yourself running a movie in your mind about not being able to do it, along with an accompanying emotion of fear or dread. Whilst you do this, you are reinforcing the neural connections in your brain that tell you that you can't do it, and strengthening that belief in your brain. But the opposite is also true. When you run a positive future scene in your mind, you are simultaneously creating the neural connections that reinforce the belief that you can do it.

There are two key factors that support the rewiring of the brain when you visualise. The first is emotion and feeling.

When visualising, there needs to be a strong emotional connection to the future picture. If you are visualising it while doubting it, or even doing so in a neutral state, it will have no effect. On the other hand, if you are visualising while simultaneously engaging an optimistic feeling that what you are visualising is going to happen, you will experience greater results.

The second factor that influences visualisation is repetition. When you visualise something new, neural connections are made. But life's challenges, particularly those that conflict with what you have visualised, can break those connections. Repeating a visualisation over and over again can stabilise the new neural connections in the brain.

Visualisation Practice

Time: 3-5 minutes

1. Sit in a quiet place where you will not be disturbed. Begin to visualise something that you would like to create or achieve.
2. Visualise with all your senses. What can you see, hear, smell, taste and touch in the image? It is important to first *see* the image clearly; if you can't, you may not be able to experience it through your other senses.
3. Ensure you are engaging your emotions. Feel what it feels like to achieve the goal you are visualising.
4. Run yourself through some actions in the 'scene'. Perhaps you are speaking in front of a large audience, perhaps you are the CEO of a corporation, or managing a large team. Experience what it is like to be your 'future self' in this situation.

5. Is there anything you can learn from this version of yourself? If there was one thing they could share with you now that would enable you to bridge the gap between where you are and where they are, what would it be?
6. End the visualisation by feeling the future picture strongly in your heart and tuning into what you are grateful for in the present that has got you to where you are now.
7. Repeat this daily for a minimum of 21 days to get results.

Weekend Mind Practices

Over the past week we have explored a range of tools for the mind. Some of these practices such as the Red Car Technique can be used any time you are triggered. But in order to develop a healthy relationship with your mind, it is essential to carry out a regular meditation practice, preferably every day. You can use the mindfulness meditation practice that we worked with this week. You can also explore some other meditation practices.

There are as many meditation practices as there are different types of food. To give you some variety from the mindfulness meditation practice, you can try using a word or sentence when you meditate. For example, as you breathe in say, "Peace," in your mind, and as you breathe out, do the same.

Some people prefer to use an affirmation or mantra that can help to have something to focus upon during meditation. As you inhale you could say something like "I breathe in peace," and as you exhale, you could say, "I breathe out peace." You can substitute any other word or phrase, but make sure it is a relaxing and calming one. It is best not to use words such as 'stress' in a practice such as this. Some people use a mantra such as "I am breathing out tension," or "I am breathing out stress," but it isn't recommended, as your body has a relationship with these words and you may subconsciously create more stress and tension in the process.

Some people like to visualise a calm or serene setting when they meditate. Although this can be helpful, it is important to note that meditation isn't so much about 'escaping to a happy place' as it is about being present. So ensure if you use this kind of practice that you aren't doing it to create more escapism.

Whichever method you choose, stick with the same method throughout the whole meditation, and try an extended meditation of 10-20 minutes this weekend.

Summary of Chapter Four

The purpose of this chapter is to give you:

- Tools to observe your thoughts and the impact they are having on your physical and emotional wellbeing
- Practices to enable you to improve mental hygiene and interrupt destructive thought processes
- An introduction to meditation and mindfulness practices that will enable you to be more present and conscious throughout your daily life, both at home and in the workplace
- Tools and processes that will enable you to adopt more positive and creative thought processes.

Summary of Practices

Monday – The Red Car

Notice when your thoughts are dragging you along. See the thought as a red car (or alternatively a train that you can't get off). Practise letting go of the thought.

Tuesday – The Space In Between Things

Notice several objects in the room and then take your attention to the space in between you and the objects.

Wednesday – Mindfulness Meditation

Sit in a comfortable position, following your breath with your eyes closed. If thoughts arise, notice them without judgement before bringing yourself back to focusing on your breathing.

Thursday – Self-talk

Observe your self-talk. If you find yourself making judgemental statements about yourself, or asking closed or conclusion-based questions, switch them into open questions about how you can experience different positive results.

Friday – Visualisation

Visualise a future goal that you would like to achieve. Ensure you visualise it with all your senses and repeat the technique regularly (for a minimum of 21 days) to get results.

Meditation

There are a variety of meditation techniques. You can repeat a word such as 'peace' or a sentence such as "I breathe in peace, I breathe out peace."

Main Outcome of This Chapter:

Aim to incorporate at least ten minutes of meditation into your daily routine from here on in, extending to fifteen the following week and twenty the week after.

CHAPTER FIVE

Relationships

In the practice of tolerance, one's enemy is the best teacher.

The Dalai Lama

How you excel or show up in the world really matters.

You have probably met some highly successful individuals who lack social or people skills. And so you've seen that success is not always dependent on how people relate to each other. However, even though we can operate in business without getting on well, interpersonal conflicts can take up time, energy and resources, and can knock us off our course as well.

A large majority of us let our moods be dictated by whether someone has pushed our buttons or not. Many of us are unaware of how much the reactions of others are affecting us. Someone says something positive and we feel good. Someone else says something negative and we chew on it all day; it distracts us from the present moment. This is such a socially acceptable pattern that we don't question it, and often aren't aware that we have any choice about it. We can literally find ourselves acting like puppets, with our strings pulled, when someone reacts in a certain way.

The most common reaction in a situation such as this is to try to control the other person to minimise the impact of how we feel. If it's a personal relationship, we might start telling our partner how they need to behave in order for us to stay with them. In a business context we might find ourselves doing something similar with our associates, collaborators or employees. We often try and control their behaviour so *we* can feel better. We may have even learnt that people will 'walk all over us' if we don't do this, and in many cases we find that our happiness depends on whether we can control the people around us to behave in a way that is acceptable to us.

Separation

This view of needing to control others comes from our culture, which teaches us that we are all separate. In many Eastern spiritual teachings, there is often a sense or belief that we are "all one" and that much less separation, or none at all, exists between individuals. From this viewpoint, there is often a common teaching of compassion, altruism, random acts of kindness, community and so on.

It can be a big leap to go from seeing everyone as separate to everyone as connected. There are, though, a number of practices and tools from Eastern philosophy and teachings that can help us to increase our compassion for the people around us, our connection with them, and our understanding of them.

The practices this week are designed to work on three levels. Firstly, they will enable you to give the people around you more compassion and understanding when you do not see eye to eye with them or when their own buttons are pushed. Secondly, they will enable you to be less likely to react to your own triggers. A socially healthy individual is not necessarily one that is never affected by others, but is instead one who knows how to handle themselves when issues arise, and this chapter will give you tools to enable you to do so. Thirdly, the practices provide tools for dealing with highly aggressive situations, enabling you to strengthen your own boundaries when you encounter someone else's extreme anger. We'll also be adding in some additional practices such as random acts of kindness, which will increase your sense of connection and feeling of wellbeing.

One other point before we go into the week. Many of the managers I work with are uncomfortable when I ask them how they interrelate with their employees. It's an area of resistance. I often hear something along the lines of "I need to be in control so that I can lead." The practices that follow will enable you to increase your leadership skills.

Organisations such as Google and Spotify understand the importance of running people-centred organisations. The old model in which employees are driven by stress and fear is being replaced by new models, which place open communication and improved interpersonal relationships at the top of the agenda. It goes without saying that happy employees who feel they are valued and understood are more productive. So, whilst these techniques are aimed at how we relate on an interpersonal level, they are also applicable to organisations and the management structures within them.

Sunday Evening Preparation

Take an overview of the way you have been reacting to others. Do you have a tendency to blame? Can you remember any instances where you tried to control others so that you could feel better? Remember, this is an opportunity to build self-awareness rather than an invitation to self-judge, so when you notice your old behaviours, it is a chance to change them.

Monday – Emptying your Emotional Bottle

- Instead of bottling up your feelings, talk them through with a friend or write them down. Often when you verbalise something, it loses its power over you. If you think back to the previous chapter, we highlighted how sometimes we can get dragged along by a red car when we are triggered. If you are experiencing a red car that you can't let go of, sometimes naming it and talking it through can diminish its power over you.
- If you are having a distressing experience, mentally replay it and look at it from the outside as an observer, as if you are watching yourself in a movie. See if you can find a different and more helpful view on what is happening.
- Ask yourself: "What can I learn from this? What might be the lesson here? What could I do differently next time?"
- Imagine yourself handling the situation differently, and getting a better outcome.
- Mentally rehearse the ways you would handle such a situation should it ever happen again.
- If you are a bit of a perfectionist and tend to be very hard on yourself, try giving yourself a break. For a few days, think of yourself as a valued friend who needs support and encouragement. If you know this "friend" is genuinely doing their best, there is nothing to be gained from constant criticism.

Even if you don't have a current conflict that you can apply the above suggestions to, consider applying them to a previous one – particularly if it still has some emotional charge for you.

Tuesday – Increasing Acceptance and Connection

Today's practices are designed to increase your levels of acceptance of others. You will find that the more you practise these tools in your interpersonal relationships, the more effective they will be.

One important note though. Increasing your acceptance doesn't mean that you are willing to let people walk all over you. There is a difference between being in acceptance of others and being a doormat to them, and these often get confused. The following statement will ensure that you are still being true to yourself when you work through the acceptance practices.

"That Isn't Going to Work for Me" (The Antidote to Blame)

As you increase your own levels of self-awareness through the tools that you use in this book, you will be getting a clearer idea of what works for you and what doesn't work for you. When you blame someone or point a finger at them, it widens the separation and increases the conflict between you. But there is a simple, non-blaming statement you can use when there is an interpersonal challenge. It is the statement: "That is not going to work for me." A blaming statement such as "You can't do that," or a command such as "Stop doing that," implies wrongness. This new statement puts the emphasis back on yourself and means you take ownership of what does and doesn't work for you.

Practice One: Active Listening

Most of us don't really listen to the person we are talking to. Instead we are mentally preparing what we are going to say whilst half-listening to the other person.

For each conversation you have today, listen attentively, refraining from trying to control the conversation or interrupting them as they speak. Paraphrase what you hear to clarify what has been said so the speaker can hear themselves too. Make a mental note of the difference this makes to the receiver. Being heard is one of our basic human needs and active listening can totally transform a personal or professional relationship.

Practice Two: Changing Places

When someone has an issue, particularly someone that you have no empathy for, imagine changing places with them in your head. Take a moment to consider their thoughts, feelings, perspective or triggers. See if you can see the world through their eyes. Return to your communication with them with this new understanding of their perspective.

Practice Three: Releasing Your Need to Be Right

If you find yourself being attached to your point of view and ready to argue the 'rightness' of it, try pausing for a moment. Notice the strong desire within yourself to be right, but instead of acting on it, sit with it with awareness for a few minutes. Notice if anything changes when you do. Go back to the situation without the attachment to defending your point of view, and see what changes.

Practice Four: Giving Praise

Various studies have highlighted that we need to have a ratio of at least five positive statements to each negative one in order for the relationship to thrive. If you have any working or personal relationships where your negative feedback outweighs your positive, try tipping the balance and looking for opportunities to praise.

Practice Five: Heart Watching

This technique is adapted from *Mind Calm* by Sandy Newbigging.[9]

Imagine that your heart has eyes. When you are communicating with someone, picture looking out at them through your heart. Practise this regularly to increase compassion and connection.

Wednesday – Dealing with Triggers

In Chapter 4 on the mind you learnt how to deal with your thoughts when they trigger you. We highlighted how many of your thoughts drag you along and how you can break the pattern with awareness, choosing not to be dragged along by them. Hopefully you have practised this several times now and started to catch yourself when you spiral into negative thinking. The practice is similar when we get triggered by someone.

This can be the most challenging thing to get our heads around, especially if we are used to blaming others for how we feel. But, on the other hand, it is also fairly liberating because it means we can take responsibility for what has been triggered in us, rather than constantly looking outside of ourselves when our buttons get pushed. This doesn't mean blaming ourselves either. In fact, dealing with your triggers can become a 'blame-free zone' when you start to take responsibility for them. You can become much more pragmatic and much less reactive when you get triggered as a result.

Exercise: When Someone Has Triggered You

Practice: Carry out the preparation for this at home and then use it if someone triggers you, either this week, or at a later date.

1. The first stage of trigger management is awareness. What are your buttons? Who or what usually presses them? Where or why did you start reacting this way? This is not about deep analysis, but rather awareness.
2. How do you usually react when you are triggered? Do you snap? Retreat into yourself and bottle up your feelings? Complain to others?
   Increase your awareness of your personal reactions.
3. What are you going to do differently next time? You now have a range of tools and techniques at your disposal that you can adapt to dealing with your triggers. The key is, if possible, to take yourself out of the current situation and change your state before you react. One suggestion is to notice the red car that you

have grabbed onto, once the trigger has been activated, and to let go. Another is to sit with your eyes closed and simply allow the frustration or anger that you are feeling to be present within you, rather than trying to resist it or push it away. Sometimes deep, intentional breathing can move the feeling that has been created. Other times you might need to shake it off from your physical body with some of the body techniques, such as jumping up and down, stamping or clapping (obviously not in front of the person who has pushed your buttons!).

4. When you have shifted yourself out of the trigger and you have moved beyond the rush of emotions that accompanied it, then reassess how to deal with the situation. Was the person truly out of order, or did they just create a reaction in you because of your triggers?

The key is to remember that you don't have to be stuck with the feeling. Be creative, try a variety of different tools, and see what helps in any given moment. Also, if you have had a lifetime of reacting to others, it can take time to catch yourself when you are triggered, and shift from projecting the blame outwards, to taking the responsibility inwards. Remember to go easy on yourself if you find yourself reacting.

Thursday – Choosing Your Company

Much of what we have highlighted in this chapter so far has been about increasing your compassion and connection with others and building bridges when conflicts occur.

Although ideally we will be able to find a bridge across all our communication and relationship challenges, we also need to know that not everyone is ready to meet us where we are. Some people are so locked behind their own filters, perspectives and points of view that connecting with them can not only be difficult, but also draining.

If you have a mission in life, goals to fulfil, and dreams to achieve, ideally you want to surround yourself with other optimists and dreamers who have a similar vision.

There are two types of behaviours that can drain your energy and take you away from your goals and dreams. They are doubters and moaners.

We have already touched upon the fact that your brain is highly programmable and the more you repeat certain thoughts or beliefs, the stronger the associated neural connections become.

We are also mirrors for one another's moods. In *The Contagious Power of Thinking*, Dr David Hamilton highlights that "Moods spread from brain to brain – not via a virus or any mysterious route, but due to the action of interconnected groups of cells in the brain called mirror neurons."[10] This is why we are affected by the moods of others and why it is beneficial to surround ourselves with people who mirror our positive moods.

Practice: Relationship Inventory

Take an inventory of all the relationships you have in your life. Are there any that are built around doubting or moaning?

It isn't necessarily about cutting these people out of your life, but rather, changing how you relate to them. Remember the statement at the start of this chapter: "That's not going to work for me." Are there any relationships where you can address what is not working for you? Remember, this is very different to controlling others or telling them how to be, or telling people what you don't like about them!

Instead, you can highlight that you want to address the patterns the relationship has fallen into so that it can develop into something healthier.

For example, "I've noticed that we've fallen into the habit of moaning together. I wonder if you would be open to us being more solution-focused in future?" (How would you say that in your own words?)

Sometimes the tone might need to be a bit firmer, particularly if someone has been doubting you or undermining you. Still, you can keep out of blaming statements: "I've noticed we have fallen into some patterns in our communication that aren't so healthy for either of us. I'd like to see if we can improve the way we are communicating so it isn't so judging or blaming." (Again, adapt this to something you would say.) Alternatively, "It just isn't working for me how we are communicating. Are you open to working on this with me so it's healthier for both of us?"

If you encounter defensiveness from the other party, remember that they may have been triggered by what you are reflecting to them. Try the Heart Watching Technique or one of the other compassion-building practices so you do not join them in the triggered state and create more conflict.

Friday – Dealing with Aggression

There may be some relationships in your work or personal life that are currently beyond conflict resolution. You may encounter authority figures, relatives, colleagues and so on who are so fixed in their current paradigm that they are not ready to meet you where you are or change their behaviour. The following two techniques will help you to remain centred even when others are aggressive or hostile, and to minimise the possibility of you becoming triggered yourself.

Whilst many of the practices in this chapter so far have increased your sense of connection, the following are designed to disconnect you from the hostility of another person.

The Bubble Technique

This is a useful technique you can teach yourself that has helped many people in situations where they have felt under pressure or have faced aggression.

1. Visualise yourself inside a bubble. Ensure that it has a colour and texture which increase your sense of safety. Now fill your bubble with all your favourite things, including music, memories, smells and feelings.

2. The surface of the bubble can protect you from negativity and aggression from outside sources. Visualise aggressive words and behaviours bouncing off or being deflected by the bubble's surface. Simultaneously the contents of the bubble can make you feel relaxed, calm, and confident, allowing you to think clearly and respond in a more assertive manner.

3. You can use the bubble technique as a meditative practice, even when you aren't anxious. Meditating in this space will increase your sense of tranquillity, making it easier to connect to the bubble when there is an aggressive conflict. Eventually you will find that you can quickly create your bubble during actual stressful events and feel safer and more confident in those situations.

Shrinking the Other Person

If there is someone who intimidates you (intentionally or not), try using your imagination to reduce your reaction.

1. Close your eyes and visualise the person standing in front of you. Now start to shrink them in the same way as can be seen in sci-fi movies.

2. Shrink them right down until they are only a few inches tall, and you have to lean forward to see them.

3. Make their voice squeaky and tiny. They will lose their power over you if you don't perceive them to be such a threat. In fact, you might realise that mentally you had been making them bigger than they actually are, and this will help to reverse that.

Weekend Practice: Random Acts of Kindness

Although we finished the working week by looking at ways you can deal with highly-charged conflicts, we want to finish this week by coming back to one of the main purposes of this chapter, which is to increase your sense of connection with those around you and move away from the idea that we are all separate.

One of the key ways to improve your sense of connection with others is through random acts of kindness. These acts of kindness have more of an effect on your health and wellbeing than you might imagine. In *Why Kindness is Good for You*, Dr David Hamilton reveals scientific evidence that kindness changes the brain, impacts the heart and immune system, and may even be an antidote to depression. He shares how we are genetically wired to be kind. When we're kind, our bodies are much healthier. Dr Hamilton's book reveals how kindness can make a damaged heart regenerate faster; how kindness and compassion alter the neural structures of our brains; and that gratitude can make you at least twenty-five per cent happier. [11]

There are a number of different ways you can engage in random acts of kindness. The most obvious one is to make a donation to charity, and if this is within your means, then it would be gratefully received. However, I also encourage you to carry out acts of kindness that involve human connection. It's one thing to make a donation to a soup kitchen and another thing entirely to look a homeless person in their eyes as you serve them their lunch.

Random acts of kindness don't need to be huge. Paying for the shopping or the coffee for the person in front of you in the queue, for example, are small acts that can have a huge impact.

Practicing random acts of kindness regularly – particularly those which you don't take credit for, or tell others about (so that you don't fall into the trap of doing them for your ego!) – will reduce your sense of separation from others, as well as make you feel good in general.

Summary of Chapter Five

Practicing the tools in this chapter will enable you to:

- Give the people around you more compassion and understanding when they are having difficult moments or when their own buttons are pushed.
- Cope with triggers, aggression and conflict in relationships.

Summary of Practices

Monday – Emptying your Emotional Bottle

Talk through your feelings or write them down. Mentally replay challenging experiences, observing them to help change perspective. Ask yourself: "What can I learn from this?" Imagine yourself handling the situation differently and mentally rehearse the new scene.

Tuesday – Increasing Acceptance and Connection

"That isn't going to work for me," is a statement you can use instead of blaming.

Active Listening – Listen attentively to conversations, refraining from interrupting.

Changing Places – When someone has an issue, particularly someone that you have no empathy for, imagine changing places with them in your head.

Releasing Your Need to Be Right – If you find yourself being attached to your point of view and ready to argue the 'rightness' of it, try sitting with the desire to be right for a few minutes and see if it diminishes.

Giving Praise – Give at least five positives to every negative.

Heart Watching – Imagine that your heart has eyes, and look out at the person you are communicating with from that perspective to increase compassion.

Wednesday – Dealing with Triggers

Become aware of when you get triggered and what your reactions are. Create a plan for when you are triggered in future. Take yourself away from the situation and change your state. If you need to deal with the person that has triggered you, do so afterwards from your calmer state.

Thursday – Choosing your Company

Take a relationship inventory. Address any differences with non-blaming statements and decide to spend time with people who mirror your vision and passion and have a calming effect on you.

Friday – Dealing with Aggression

Bubble Technique – Create a bubble around you when you encounter violence and aggression. Fill it with all the things that make you feel safe.

Shrinking the Other Person – If you encounter aggression from someone, imagine them shrinking and their voice diminishing.

Main Outcome of This Chapter:

Ensure that you have tools for dealing with your own triggers and also the triggers that occur outside of you. Increase activities that improve your compassion for others and practise them regularly.

This will help to improve and enhance the quality of your working and personal relationships.

CHAPTER SIX

Why Use These Tools? Evidence and Research

The point of power is always in the present moment.

Louise L. Hay

Many of the techniques in this book have become popular in the workplace in the US over the past decade, and are becoming increasingly popular in the UK – and globally. Google searches for the term 'mindfulness' have more than doubled in the past five years. This means that there is a body of evidence to support the practices within this book. You can carry out the techniques without examining this research, but if you are the type of person that needs scientific proof before you engage in something, the following research will show you why it is worth engaging the next twenty-eight days of your life in learning these techniques and using them on a daily basis after that.

Search Inside Yourself

One of the most compelling studies on how these and similar tools can be used across the board in the workplace comes from Google. To promote innovation, engineers at Google are given twenty per cent of their time to develop projects outside of their work that support their productivity and creativity in the workplace. One of Google's engineers, Chade-Meng Tan, developed a project called *Search Inside Yourself*. His diverse group included a Stanford University scientist, a Zen Master, a CEO, and Daniel Goleman (who wrote *the* book on emotional intelligence).

In his book, *Search Inside Yourself*, Tan highlights the effects that this project had on Google employees:

At work, some participants have found meaning and fulfilment in their jobs (we even had one person reverse her decision to leave Google after taking Search Inside

Yourself!), *while some have become much better at what they do.* [12]

Tan highlights numerous case studies, such as the engineering manager who reduced his working week to four days to give himself more quality time and was subsequently promoted.[13] He achieved the art that many of us secretly dream of: achieving more whilst doing less.

Another sales engineer at the company found that the project helped him become more credible to his customers. He reportedly became "better at calmly overcoming objections during product demonstrations" as well as speaking "compassionately about competitors" and being "courageous and truthful" when telling customers about Google's products.[14] If you think of what we highlighted about fearing the future, it seems that the courage that Tan describes actually means that the sales engineer was no longer fearing a future outcome while selling. The project appears to have taken him out of his mind and into the present moment so that he had the resourcefulness to adapt to his customers, rather than blindly following a script or placating them with what he thought they wanted to hear. The same kind of resourcefulness and engagement to the present moment can be achieved by carrying out the practices in this book.

But it isn't just Google who have innovated mindfulness practices in their company. Barclays, Deutsche Bank, Apple, Yahoo, KPMG and Starbucks are just some of the companies who have invested in similar training for their employees, with outstanding results.

Global Research on Mindfulness and Meditation Practices

There have been over 2,500 global scientific research studies, which have unanimously revealed the advantages of the mindfulness process. These include studies carried out by Harvard University.

Evidence-based studies have highlighted the benefits of mindfulness in the workplace, including a greater sense of wellbeing and a greater sense of corporate responsibility.

On an individual level, cognitive function is improved – including the ability to concentrate, learn, create and remember. Employees become more productive, and have a heightened sense of wellbeing.

For the corporation, this means benefits such as enhanced job satisfaction and a lower staff turnover. Staff absenteeism is reduced – including absenteeism caused by illness and injury as well as stress. As we saw earlier with the study at Google, client relationships also improve, alongside the ability to communicate effectively on an inter- and intrapersonal level. [15]

Meditation and the Brain

In order to understand why these results are being achieved, it helps to have an overview of the impact that meditation has on the brain. A regular meditation practice has been shown to change the shape of the brain. Electroencephalography (EEG) has been used in many studies to define the activity of the meditating brain. The primary purpose of using EEG in meditation is to determine its effect on the cerebral cortex. The cerebral cortex is the part of the brain responsible for decision-making, attention and memory. An EEG can measure the activity of different brain waves (delta, beta, theta and alpha).

In a 2006 study, Cahn and Polich linked increased alpha and theta brain waves to meditation.[16] Alpha brain waves heighten imagination, memory, learning and concentration. Theta brain waves are associated with inspiration, creativity and insight. When alpha and theta waves meet one another, the creative power of the mind is enhanced.

Improving your own brainwave activity means that you are more readily able to access these abilities of the brain on a moment-to-moment basis.

Another study by Sara Lazar, a research scientist at Massachusetts General Hospital, showed that the grey matter of twenty men and women who meditated for forty minutes per day was thicker than that of people who did not.[17] This change was in the part of the brain that affected decision-making, attention and memory. What was interesting about the research carried out in Massachusetts General is, unlike previous studies on meditation which had focused on Zen monks, the study was carried out on Boston workers practicing a Western style of meditation. Researchers at Harvard, Yale, and the Massachusetts Institute of Technology also confirmed that meditation alters the physical structure of the brain.

Lowering Stress

If you have been stressed, your sympathetic nervous system will have been overactive. An increase in sympathetic nervous system activity means you have more blood in your arms and legs (preparing you to fight or flee). Stimulation of the sympathetic nervous system increases the amount of adrenaline in your body, also preparing you to fight or flee. Some of the many side effects of too much adrenaline in the body include nervousness, insomnia and lowered immunity.

Most of the tools in this book stimulate the parasympathetic nervous system, which enables the body to rest, digest and heal. Practices such as meditation take our body and our mind from a place of hyperactivity, fear, unrest and uneasiness to a state of inner calm, peace and silence.

Other studies have shown how mindfulness practices lower the stress hormone, cortisol. In the introduction to this book we highlighted how stress is one of the biggest challenges that we face in the modern world. In a study by the University of California, Davis found that mindfulness practices such as meditation and breathing techniques that focus on the present moment, like the ones presented in this book, can lower the levels of stress hormones in the body. The findings were published in *Health Psychology*.[18]

Implementation of Meditation and Mindfulness in the Work Environment

Meditation has a general impact in the workplace and it also has a place in the development of leadership. A study carried out by A.D. Amar *et al.* at the University of Westminster measured the self-perception of leadership skills among a sample of senior managers in the London area. The study then put them through a 12-week meditation programme (using a technique called Vipassana meditation).

The results were published in the *Academy of Management Proceedings.* Overall, their self-confidence, shared vision and moral intelligence were said to improve. [19]

Implementing This Research in Your Daily Life

While the research presented in this chapter may be impressive, it is the implementation of these practices in your daily life that will help you see these results.

Summary of Chapter Six

The benefits in the workplace of mindfulness and meditation – and related techniques such as the ones presented in this book – include a greater sense of wellbeing and a greater sense of corporate responsibility.

Cognitive function is improved – including the ability to concentrate, learn, create and remember. Employees become more productive, and have a heightened sense of wellbeing.

Meditation increases alpha brain waves, heightening imagination, memory, learning and concentration. It also positively impacts theta brain waves that are associated with inspiration, creativity and insight.

The techniques in this book will stimulate the parasympathetic nervous system, which enables the body to rest, digest and heal. Practices such as meditation take our body and our mind from a place of hyperactivity, fear, unrest and uneasiness to a state of inner calm, peace and silence.

Conclusion

Putting it All Together

No one can get inner peace by pouncing on it.
Harry Emerson Fosdick

By now you have experienced a range of techniques that have hopefully changed your relationship with your breathing, mind, and body, as well as the way you relate to others.

Going through the four-week programme is already a significant achievement, whether you have just practised a small number of the practices or attempted every single one in this book.

The programme was structured to take you on a journey and each practice was designed to unfold from the next. What is crucial at this stage is that, now you have completed the four weeks, you continue to use these tools in a dynamic way, and that you integrate them into your daily routine.

They are skills you can use throughout your lifetime to maintain a calm, productive, fulfilling and meaningful existence.

As human beings, we have a tendency to engage in a particular programme while it is in the forefront of our minds, and then to forget what we have learnt in the face of our everyday pressures. There is a reason for this. Remember how we highlighted that the more you repeat a habit, the stronger the neural connection in the brain becomes? Whilst you are repeating the exercises in this programme, you are strengthening the neural connections associated with them; put the programme aside for a few weeks, and the techniques could easily be forgotten.

We want to ensure that you make a habit of using at least some of the tools presented in this book, as they will only have an impact on reducing your stress levels if they are practised regularly and repeated often.

Remember: Retest your blood pressure with your doctor so that you can measure the impact of the programme so far. Also, repeat the WEMWBS and the GAD-7 test which we presented in the first chapter.

You may recall that, in Chapter 1, we mentioned the Apex Effect, which is common in therapy. This is where an issue has been transformed and the client forgets how bad it was in the first place. If you have practised the programme for four weeks, you may have forgotten where you started, so retest to give yourself a measure of your success.

The effects of establishing a regular practice that includes daily meditation and mindfulness exercises, supported by breath and body work, will continue to have a cumulative impact on your health and wellbeing, changing your whole perspective and outlook. You will not only be stress-free in the workplace, but will know how to manage and transform stress in all other areas of your life too.

Remember these are skills you can now use for the rest of your life.

Also by Hansa Pankhania:
From Stress to Success: *Five Inspirational Stories of Overcoming Workplace Stress*

Whatever your situation, I feel confident that you will find something in this book that will unleash positive changes in your work and home life in powerful ways.
This collection of workplace short stories is written from experience, and inspired by our clients. These stories are based on scenarios and interventions which will resonate with you and give you tips and techniques to help you overcome common, as well as complex, workplace issues. The combination makes this an interesting and exciting read.
In this book you will find:

* Resilience Building - Discover expert techniques that will enable you to thrive during difficult challenging times
* Change Management - Learn how to derive positive outcomes from difficult change
* Anger Management - Avoid letting your anger compromise your relationships and career
* Stress Management - Learn how to overcome stressful situations and avoid a breakdown
* Mediation - Find out how to resolve conflict in the workplace

This book is based upon real-life situations and interventions. It is packed full of advice on how to overcome stress and perform at your peak, despite challenges. Each story is accompanied by a commentary, with expert guidance and tips.

Acknowledgements

I am eternally grateful:

To all my loving family and friends for their faith and patience in my projects

To my clients, for the opportunity to learn and grow and make a difference

To my intern, Ellie Hawkins for researching and collating the initial material for this book

To my Associates, for supporting and sharing my vision

To my editor, Lois Rose, for her expertise, wisdom, guidance and encouragement

To the Almighty, for the strength and courage to follow my path.

About the Author

Hansa Pankhania is a Corporate Wellbeing Consultant, Trainer, Executive Coach and Speaker. She has worked with over one hundred companies, helping managers and employees to reduce stress and build resilience.
She is a Fellow of the International Stress Management Association.
Contact: hansa@aumconsultancy.co.uk

Bibliography

Cantore, Stefan, and Passmore, Jonathan. *Top Business Psychology Models*. London: Kogan Page, 2012.

Chopra, Deepak. *Seven Spiritual Laws of Success*. London: Transworld Pubs, 2007.

Dave, N.V. *Vedanta and Management*. New Delhi: Deep & Deep Publications, 1997.

Dobson, C.B. *Stress- The Hidden Adversary*. Lancaster: MTP Press Ltd, 1982.

Duddy, Barry. *Personal Best*. UK: Vencape, 2012.

Goleman, Daniel. *Healing Emotions*. Boston: Shambhala, 1997.

McGuigan, F.J. *Encyclopedia of Stress*. USA: Allyn and Bacon, 1999.

Meichenbaum, Donald. *Stress Inoculation Training*. USA: Allyn and Bacon, 1985.

Nayar, Vineet. *Employees First - Customers Second*. Boston: Harvard Business Press, 2010.

Palmer, Stephen, and Cooper, Cary. *How To Deal With Stress*. London: Kogan Page, 2013.

Palmer, Stephen, and Dryden, Windy. *Counselling for Stress Problems*. London: Sage Publications Ltd, 1995.

Shaffer, Martin, PhD. *Life After Stress*. New York: Plenum Press, 1982.

Tan, Chade-Meng. *Search Inside Yourself*. London: HarperCollins, 2012.

Tolle, Eckhart. *The Power of Now*. California, USA: New World Library, 1999.

Wilson, Kevin. *Project Bloom*. UK: Equinox One Publishing, 2012.

Woolfolk, Robert L., and Lehrer, Paul M. *Principles and Practices of Stress Management*. London: Guildford Press, 1984.

References

[1] Taken from the ancient yoga text, *Hatha Yoga Pradipka*

[2] http://www.stress.org/take-a-deep-breath/

[3] See The American Institute of Stress http://www.stress.org/take-a-deep-breath/ for more information.

[4] The study, which was funded by the National Institutes of Health, appears in the July/August 2002 issue of *Psychosomatic Medicine*. Source: http://corporate.dukemedicine.org/news_and_publications/news_office/news/5687

[5] See *Earthing: The Most Important Health Discovery Ever?* Ober, Clinton, Sinatra, Stephen T. MD, Zucker, Martin.

[6] Journal of Applied Physiology 49(5): 881-887, 1980. Journal of Applied Physiology 49(5): 881-887, 1980 at http://jap.physiology.org/content/49/5/881.abstract

[7] Newbigging, Sandy, *Thunk!*, Forres, UK, Findhorn Press Ltd, 2012, p.10.

[8] Newbigging, Sandy C., *Thunk!* p. 39.

[9] Newbigging, Sandy C., *Mind Calm*, Hay House, p. 167.

[10] Hamilton, David R., *The Contagious Power of Thinking*, Hay House, London, 2011, p. 2.

[11] Hamilton, David R., *Why Kindness is Good For You*, Hay House, London, 2010.

[12] Tan, Chade-Meng, *Search Inside Yourself*, [Kindle 209]

[13] Tan, Chade-Meng, *Search Inside Yourself*, [Kindle 209]

[14] Tan, Chade-Meng, *Search Inside Yourself*, [Kindle 214]

[15] Summary of the research of the American Institute of Health, University of Massachusetts, and the Mind/Body Medical Institute at Harvard University.

[16] Cahn BR, Polich J (2006), "Meditation states and traits: EEG, ERP, and neuroimaging studies". Psychological Bulletin 132 (2): 180–211. doi:10.1037/0033-2909.132.2.180. PMID 16536641.]

[17] Lazar, Sara PhD., "Mindfulness Meditation Training Changes Brain Structure in 8 Weeks", January 30 2011, *Psychiatry Research: Neuroimaging,* study led by Massachusetts General Hospital, Psychiatric Neuroimaging Research Program.

[18] *HealthPsychology,* http://davidbridwell.info/papers/Jacobs_Self_reported_mindfulness_and_cortisol.pdf

[19] You can see a summary of this study on http://greatergood.berkeley.edu/article/item/three_benefits_to_mindfulness_at_work

NOTES

NOTES

NOTES

NOTES

NOTES

NOTES

NOTES